ECHOES FROM THE OLD TESTAMENT

Wisdom for Teens

Quinn Morris, Psy.D.

Order this book online at www.trafford.com
or email orders@trafford.com

Most Trafford titles are also available at major online book retailers.

Printed in Victoria, BC, Canada.

ISBN: 978-1-4269-2973-1 (sc)

*Our mission is to efficiently provide the world's finest, most comprehensive book publishing
service, enabling every author to experience success. To find out how to publish your
book, your way, and have it available worldwide, visit us online at www.trafford.com*

Trafford rev. 3/18/2010

 www.trafford.com

North America & international
toll-free: 1 888 232 4444 (USA & Canada)
phone: 250 383 6864 ♦ fax: 812 355 4082

Bible References
KJV – King James Version
NKJV – New King James Version
NIV – New International Version
NAS – New American Standard
NAB – New Catholic Answer Bible
Amplified Bible
The Message Bible
NLT – New Living Translation Bible

ACKNOWLEDGEMENTS

Thanks be to God for everything that He has done for me and for His inspiration. Thanks to Anita Siler who took out the time to edit this book through many changes and to John Siler for encouraging me to get started and to persist in my endeavor.

DEDICATION

This book is dedicated to my mother who told me that I should write a book, to my husband, who encouraged me every step of the way and to my daughter and son, whom I love very much.

CONTENTS

INTRODUCTION

Too many times when we read the Bible, we feel that those things that happened so many years ago have very little, if anything, to do with what is happening today. There are also others who think that the Bible is full of fairy tales. Yet, the Bible is still the most widely read book today.

Many of us go to church every week and listen to the preached message about different events in the Bible, and how they were handled by the people of that day. Among other things, these people are often presented as brave, strong, persistent, faithful, obedient, and receiving divine rewards. But church leaders also teach us about the people's disobedience, their pride, their stubbornness, and their punishments.

Wouldn't it be interesting if we could just sit down and talk with some of those Biblical characters today? Think of the many questions that could be asked, or the conversations we could have with them about some of the events in their lives. It would be wonderful to hear them talk about themselves in their own way, the feelings that they had, the thoughts that were in their minds, the emotions that they were exhibiting, along with so many other things. They might even talk about the reasons why they did what they did.

We could tell them how we felt when we read or heard their story. It could also be an opportunity to let them hear our perspective on their life experiences. This could also give us a chance to talk about ourselves. We could tell them a little about our lives and about the world as it is today. This would be a very interesting conversation that might easily benefit all of us in our daily lives.

In an effort to provide such an opportunity, ECHOES FROM the OLD TESTAMENT WISDOM FOR TEENS, is_based on both fact and fiction, will take you back in time to present an overview of several outstanding women in the Bible. As a reader, you will have the opportunity to learn about their lives and the times in which they lived. It will also help you to understand how these Biblical women would answer some questions you might have about their lives. And wouldn't it be wonderful to hear their perception of the things that you are going through today?

Each of the following chapters will present a short outline or narrative of a significant Biblical character. This narrative or outline will be followed by various questions from young people, such as you, regarding that Bible story, along with responses from that character.

EVE

A woman of unique distinction

(Genesis 2-3)

"And the Lord God said, It is not good that man should be alone; I will make him a helper comparable to him. And the Lord God caused a deep sleep to fall on Adam, and he slept; and He took one of his ribs, and closed up the flesh in its place;"

Genesis 2:18, 21 (NJKV)

Eve was called a woman because she was taken from a man. Woman is a generic designation associated with her relation to Adam, a relation she was created to fulfill. Literally, woman means "man-ess." Her name means, "Mother of all living." It describes her function and destiny in the spiritual history of which she was the beginning. Eve literally means "life," "life giving," or "mother of all who have life," and her life is in all of us.

Eve was distinct in many ways from all other women who have ever lived because there were many firsts in her life. She was the first woman ever to live on the earth. She was never a child, a daughter, or a maiden. She was not born, but created by God. She was the first to be called a wife, to become a man's counterpart and companion. She was called a helpmeet in the scripture, giving woman her position in the world. She was the prettiest woman that the world has ever known. She was created by a perfect God and reflected His divine perfection. She was the first woman who came into this world without sin. At the time she was created, she did not even realize that there could be evil in the world. You see, she lived in a sinless world because there was no inherited sin at this time.

Eve lived with Adam in the Garden of Eden for some time. They were in charge of the animals and vegetations. God had told Adam that they were to eat from all the glorious trees in Eden, except they could not eat the fruit of the tree of knowledge of good and evil. There was no need for clothing, and they were the only two people in the garden at the time.

She then became the world's first woman sinner and introduced it to her offspring. When Satan came to her in the form of a snake and began to talk to her about the tree of knowledge of good and evil, she listened to what it had to say. The fruit on the tree was beautiful to the eye, and it looked delicious. After he had finished telling her the good qualities of the fruit, Eve had a strong desire to taste it. The snake kept encouraging her to try the fruit, making it sound better than anything that she had ever tasted before. She saw the fruit, coveted it, and she took it. She may not have even understood what the snake was telling her, because she did not know the meaning of the words wise or evil. She was so naïve that she listened to the flattering words and yielded to them. After tasting the fruit, she had to share it with Adam because she did not want to eat something that tasted that good and not share it with the only other human alive, her husband.

Eve did not realize that she was naked until after Adam had eaten the fruit from the tree. Remember, the command was given to him and not to her, therefore, God's command was not broken until after Adam had tasted the fruit. Then after eating the forbidden fruit, they tried to hide themselves when they heard the voice of God. When God found them, He asked them why they did not answer Him. They said that they were afraid to show themselves because they were naked. God asked them how they knew that they were naked, and they told Him about eating the fruit from the tree of the knowledge of good and evil. God was very angry, and made them clothing out of animal skins. He told them that Adam was going to have to become a farmer in order to take care of Eve, and that she would become pregnant and have children with great pain. He then threw them out of the garden and placed angel guards at the gate so that they could not return.

Soon after this, Eve became pregnant with her first child, Cain. She remembered what God had told her about having children, but she didn't know it was going to be so painful. She did not understand what pain was until she had Cain. She was the first woman to go through the agony of childbirth. Soon afterwards, she had another son by the name of Abel. When they grew up, Cain became a farmer and Abel was a shepherd. They had been taught about God all of their lives and knew about burnt offerings. When God accepted Abel's sacrifice and not Cain's, Cain became so jealous that he killed Abel. Eve was very upset when she found out that Abel had been killed by his own brother. This was the first murder.

Eve then experienced the meaning of death when she stood at the grave and buried her second son, Abel. She became the first mother to suffer the agony of losing a child. When Cain did not return home, she was again grief stricken. She had lost her sons, one to death and one because God had banished Cain from his family since he had committed murder. In coming years though, Eve was to be blessed in that she had many more children.

Through this woman, God's fair universe was blighted, and it became a world of sinners, lost and ruined by one fall, the fall of Adam.

If you could ask Eve a question, what would you ask?

QUESTIONS:

Kellie: What did you like best about the Garden of Eden?

Eve: I liked its beauty and tranquility. There was so much peace there. The multitudes of plants with the many colors (reds, yellows, greens, blues, purples, etc.) were magnificent. There were all kinds of animals that roamed around together. The colors of the birds and the fishes were wonderful to see. The animals would walk up to you and let you pet them, and they would eat right out of your hands. I had the opportunity to walk around the garden with Adam while he named everything. The food was delicious. I could eat anything that I wanted. There were so many choices. In fact, I could do anything that I wanted to do, and I really enjoyed myself.

Kent: How did it feel being able to talk directly with God?

Eve: It was a very unique experience. I was at peace. When we talked, I was very content. I was created from what God had already refined. I was fashioned by the hand of God from the living tissue of Adam. I had an intimate relationship with God. I knew that whatever He said was all right. I knew that God was there for me, no matter what the situation. It was wonderful.

John: Along those same lines, how did you feel talking to God after eating the forbidden fruit?

Eve: There was a great difference. I felt shame. I had come to understand the difference between good and evil. I knew that I had done wrong even listening to the serpent in the first place. Then to yield t temptation, I was so ashamed. When God called me that evening, I knew that I was in trouble. I was like many of you today, I had my excuses ready. But what I did not realize was that, with God, excuses just don't work. If you are disobedient, be ready to accept the consequences, because you just can't escape it.

Irene: Why did you eat of the fruit in the first place?

Eve: Remember, I told you how beautiful all the fruit in the garden was. Well, the fruit on the tree of knowledge of "good and evil" was the prettiest. Just to look at it brought about imagination on my part as to how good it must taste. When the serpent began to talk to me, he just whetted my appetite. During my walks in the garden with Adam, I had admired the tree and had spoken to Adam about it. Adam always reminded me about God's instructions, and I would listen to him. This did not stop me from being curious. The serpent caught me at one of my weakest moments. I was standing by the tree, looking at the fruit, when the serpent walked up to me. Don't forget, in my day, he could walk upright. It was as if he were watching and waiting for me. He sneaked up on me, and I was not aware of his presence until he spoke to me. He started out being friendly. Also, remember, all the animals were on a friendly basis, so I did not expect anything else. He began to ask questions about the fruit on the tree. He talked about its beauty. He wondered about its taste. He asked me if I had ever tasted it, and when I told him no, he began to make statements like, "It looks so good that it must also taste good." When I told him that God said that we were not to eat of the tree, I had added the word *touch* as well, and that is all he needed. He knew what God had said, and he knew that I had told a half-truth. I had added to the words of God. He began to explain to me what God really meant. He also told me the advantages that I would have if I ate of the fruit. The idea that I would be as wise as God was hard to imagine. Also, the fact that I would know right from wrong was more than I could grasp. He kept on talking about how good the fruit would taste, smacking his lips, and I just had to try it for myself. When I took a bite, it was delicious.

Marie: Why did you give Adam a piece of the fruit?

Eve: Since there was no other human being with whom to share it, I wanted Adam to taste it also. All I could think of was how good it was. I convinced Adam to try it, using my feminine wiles. He was very reluctant at first, because it was not anything that he was used to eating. He even questioned me about where I had found it. I only told him about the taste. I wanted him to experience the flavor that was like no other. He finally did as I asked, and tasted the fruit.

Marie: When did you realize that you had done wrong?

Eve: I realized it was wrong when Adam took a bite of the fruit. Suddenly there was an atmosphere of dread. I looked around and saw things differently. The beauty was still there, but my knowledge of what I had done was horrifying. At that time, I knew that I had done something wrong. I became aware of the fact that I was naked, and tried to hide myself from Adam. I also understood that I had been tricked by the serpent. I did not like the way I was feeling. These were new feelings, ones of sadness, disgust, frustration, humiliation and fear. I was hoping that God would not make His regular visit that evening, but to no avail.

Kellie: What was your relationship like with Adam before and after the fall.

Eve: Before the fall, it was perfect. My marriage had no discord. I was happy and content. After the fall, everything seemed to go wrong. My eyes were opened and I knew that we had been walking around all the time with no clothes on. This made me feel very ashamed. Adam and I had many arguments. He would blame God for giving him a woman, and then blame me for giving him the piece of fruit. Anytime one blames the other for something in a relationship, there is a problem.

Alice: How did you feel when God caught you after eating the forbidden fruit?

Eve: I felt terrible. I thought that I had gotten away with the deception, so when I heard His voice, I tried to hide myself. I felt even worse for Adam because, after all, it was I who enticed him to try the fruit. It had slipped my mind about how powerful God is. God knew that I had done something wrong even before He came to the garden that evening. I guess I was in a state of denial. I knew that I had done wrong, but I was ashamed to admit it.

John: How did you feel when God told you that you could no longer live in the garden?

Eve: I was heartbroken, angry with myself, angry with Adam, angry with the serpent, and angry with God. I knew that I had no reason to be angry with anyone but myself, but deep down I blamed Adam. He was supposed to be the head after all. He didn't have to eat the fruit just because I offered it to him. There are many other things that he did not allow me to do, so why did he listen to me this time? I blamed the serpent because he convinced me that I should taste the fruit. He knew that I was vulnerable and took advantage of it. I blamed God because He was the One who put the serpent in the garden. Why did He do such a thing? After all, we were supposed to be in charge of everything in the garden, including the animals. God knew that the serpent was bad and did not deserve to be in such a beautiful place. It was mainly His fault. I also blamed God because I thought that He would have given us another chance. I didn't believe that He was forgiving enough. You see, I just couldn't blame the person who was really at fault, me! I'm the one who started it all. It was because of me that we no longer live in the Garden of Eden. I was the one who was responsible, the guilty party, and the sinner.

Kent: In your opinion, what was the impact of your fall from grace?

Eve: Physical: The pain of childbearing Psychological: God was no longer first in my life; my desire for my husband took His place. Also, I found myself trying to please my husband. Women are doing the same thing today, as well as trying to please those who are not their husbands. They do things to bring attention to themselves. ocial: There are many men who, to this day, believe that they are the dominant ones, and that the women should be the submissive ones. This is taught and demonstrated in the family, on the job, and in some churches. Spiritual: I lost sight of whom I had been created to be. God was no longer first in my life. Women are even now being held back in some churches, and often they are not permitted to use their gifts to enrich the church.

Alice: Because of you and your sin, we women have pain, some more than others during childbirth. What did you think about the pain that you had when you gave birth to your first son, Cain?

Eve: I did not know what pain was until I gave birth to Cain. It was beyond anything that I ever imagined. Remember, we did not have the medical advantages that you have to-day. There was no anesthetic for the pain. I did not know anything about your Lamaze procedure. There were no hospitals, no doctors, no midwives, nothing. I was alone with Adam, and he did not know what to do. I had to do it all by myself, using my own instinctive reactions. It was hard. It was very, very hard, but I did it and I was very proud of myself. When I saw my baby, I was excited just knowing that he came from me. It was a miracle. I am sorry that so many women have to endure pain in childbirth, but when they see their child, I am sure they feel like I did. The pain was worth it.

Kent: What was your reaction to the death of your second son, Abel?

Eve: I was horrified. I knew that animals died, because we ate them. We had to eat something, and Abel was very good at providing us with meat. But I had never seen a human being die. When I found out that Abel was dead, something inside of me died also. He was my son, my second son. He was a part of me. I thought that I had suffered enough. I could no longer live in the garden where there was peace and quiet. I had to learn the meaning of pain. I had to work in the home, while Adam worked the land. I was losing my beauty. Hadn't I had enough hardships? God was not through with me yet.

Irene: What about Cain? How did you feel about him killing his brother?

Eve: This was very hard for me to understand. After all, I thought that we were a close family. We only had each other. I did not know that there was any jealousy between my sons. They played together when they were younger. They had their disagreements, but I did not think anything of them. What was I to know? I didn't know anything about children. I thought I was doing a good job. When I found out that Cain had killed Abel, I was devastated. While I grieved over the loss of Abel, I still loved Cain; after all, he was my firstborn son. He had done wrong, but he was still my son.

Kellie: It must have been very hard for you. You lost one son to death and the other son to exile. What were your feelings at the time?

Eve: I was traumatized. I had lost two sons. I was never to see them again. They were never going to be with me again. I became depressed. I did not want to be touched. I didn't want to be bothered. I refused to do anything. I cried a lot and I did not seem to be able to stop myself. I tried to get over that feeling, but it was very hard. I felt like I wanted to die. I thought that I had nothing to live for. I had given up.

Kellie: What advice could you give us today?

Eve: I have several pieces of advice for you in today's world.

- My first piece of advice to you would be to be obedient to God. There are many things that we could avoid if we would just obey. When I think of all the things that happened to me because of my disobedience, I am appalled. I exchanged an easy way of life for a hard one. I lost my innocence and became very experienced. I learned many things that I did not want to learn. I lost many precious things and much of my self respect because of disobedience. (To obey is better than sacrifice, and to heed is better than the fat of the rams. I Samuel 15:22b NIV)
- The second piece of advice would be to be content with what you have. There is a saying that "The grass is greener on the other side." This is not true. If you have love and security, be happy with it. If you have a family, take care of it. If you are a parent, love your children and do your best for them. Teach them the meaning of compassion, responsibility, love and respect. Take care of your home and everything that is in it, and be happy doing it. (Keep your lives free from the love of money and be content with what you have, because God has said, "Never will I leave you; never will I forsake you. Hebrews 13:5 NIV)
- The third piece of advice is to love the Lord. God should be the main Person in your life. If He is first in your life, you will be at peace. Things will not go your way all the time, or the way you think they should go, but you will have peace of mind because you know that God is working things out in His own way, and that you are willing to accept His will. (Jesus said unto him. Thou shalt love the Lord thy God with all thy heart, and with all thy soul, and with all thy mind. Matthew 22:37 KJV)

- My fourth piece of advice is to do all you can to tell the truth, even when it hurts. God knew that I had done wrong. He knew that I had listened to the serpent. He knew what he would find when he came into the garden to talk to us, but I was afraid to tell the truth. Don't be afraid to tell the truth. (And you shall know the truth, and the truth shall make you free. John 8:32 NKJV)

- My final piece of advice is to accept responsibility for your own actions. Don't try to put the blame on someone else. There should be no one who can make you do anything that you do not want to do. They can try to influence you, but you are the one who makes the final decision. Face up to this fact, and you will be a better person for it. Don't forget that God gave you the capacity to think, to remember, to be able to distinguish right from wrong, and to make decisions and choose whether or not you should act upon them. If you remember nothing else, do know that God loves you more than you can ever imagine. (So then, everyone of us shall give an account of himself to God. Romans 14:12 NIV)

HANNAH

The woman who personifies ideal motherhood

(I Samuel 1-2:11)

"And she said, O my lord! As thy soul lives, my lord, I am the woman who stood by you here praying, to the Lord. For this child I prayed, and the Lord has granted me my petition which I asked of Him. Therefore I also have lent him to the Lord; as long as he lives he shall be lent to the Lord. So they worshipped the Lord there."

(I Samuel 1:26-28 (NJKV)

Hannah was the favorite wife of Elkanah, a Levite of Ramathaim Zophim, a most honorable family. She was very unhappy because she was not able to have children. She would cry often, and each time her husband would try to comfort her, but to no avail. She went to the temple to pray on many occasions, asking God for a son. Her prayers were fervent, and she would experience God's peace while waiting for an answer from the Lord. When she returned home, there were times when she became depressed. You see, Hannah had a rival. Elkanah had another wife who would parade her children in front of Hannah whenever she could. Her husband did not blame Hannah for not having children, even though the blame was traditionally placed on the woman because she was considered cursed. This often led to divorce.

Hannah continued to make annual treks to Shiloh to worship God, even though God had not answered her prayers. When she was there she would cry out to the Lord, persistently asking Him for a child. Sometimes she would stay at the altar all day and not eat. The priest, Eli, thought that she was ill or out of her head because he noticed her at the altar moving her lips, without hearing words. She made a vow to God that if He would give her a child, she would give the child back to Him.

Hannah's sorrow was profound during those initial years of her marriage. She had a devout husband who loved her and bestowed rich gifts on her, yet her greatest burden was her barrenness. Hannah was a noble woman with inner serenity. She had a sensitive face which reflected her moods. Her character was truly unblemished. She demonstrated devotion, godliness, trust, patience, and self-sacrifice, while she continued to cry out day and night to her God because she believed that He would hear her. And God did hear her, and gave her a son whom she named Samuel. Then, as promised, she gave her son back to God when she weaned him, and visited him once a year. Later, she herself was able to give Elkanah five more children.

There remained a deep rivalry between her and Elkanah's other wife, but Hannah manifested the grace of self-control. Peninnah, the other wife, was very cruel with her reproaches and rebukes. Yet, Hannah opened her heart to God even with her sorrowful spirit, and she was never guilty of any unwomanly conduct.

Finally, one must look again at her supplication, her prayer life. While she was childless, Hannah still fervently believed in God. Her pain consistently found refuge in God's house. She so longed for motherhood that she made the vow to God that she would give her child back to Him if He would grant her one. Then, in the presence of God, she would express her sorrow with a heartfelt cry. The prayer itself seemed to be internal, as she would pray, but no sound would come from her lips. She breathed a wish directly to God, and fervently believed that God would bless her with a son, which He did. Thereupon, her prayer became a song: she offered a psalm of thanksgiving by bursting into a song of gratitude for God's goodness, divine attributes of power, holiness, knowledge, majesty, and grace.

What questions do you have for Hannah?

QUESTIONS:

John: Why did you want children?

Hannah: In my day, a woman was considered to be cursed if she did not have children. I did not feel I was cursed, and I wanted to give my husband a son.

Kellie: Was there a time when you felt that God was not listening to you?

Hannah: Yes, there was. It seemed to me like the more I prayed, the less He listened. Also, the harder I prayed the less attention He paid to me. Sometimes I would get frustrated and just break down in tears. I would ask God, why aren't you listening to me? Why can't you hear me? Why won't you answer me? What is wrong with me? I'm doing all that I can, and yet I am still not getting anywhere. What is wrong with me?

Maria: Were you excited when you became pregnant?

Hannah: I was ecstatic. God had answered my prayers. I was going to have a baby. I would no longer be considered cursed. Peninnah could no longer criticize me. I was her equal.

Alice: Why did you make a promise to God that you would give the baby back to Him?

Hannah: I felt that if I could bargain with God, I would have a better chance of having a baby. I was determined to have a child, even if I had to give it up soon after it was born. I would at least have an opportunity to visit him once a year at the temple.

Kellie: How did it feel leaving your son with Eli?

Hannah: I was a typical mother. It was hard for me to do it, but I made a vow to the Lord, and I could not go back on my vow. I was very unhappy though, and I kept thinking that Samuel was too young for me to leave him. After all, I had just weaned him and he was still only a baby. Could Eli take care of him? Who would feed him? Who would keep him clean? All these questions, and more, kept running through my head. I was worried.

Irene: How do you think you would have felt if you had not had any more children?

Hannah: I had only asked God for one child. I think I would have been satisfied with only one child, because God had granted my request. It would not have been the same as having children in my home all the time, but the knowledge that I had one child would have sufficed. I am very happy that the Lord blessed me with five more children. My house was then full of laughter and noise.

Kent: Your husband showed you from the start that he loved you very much, why weren't you satisfied?

Hannah: I was content with the fact that my husband loved me. I was happy to receive his gifts of love. The inadequacy was not in him, it was in me. I am the one who was not satisfied with me. I did not feel that I deserved him because I could not give him a son. It was all me.

Maria: Why did you tolerate the way your husband's other wife treated you?

Hannah: Well, she gave Elkanah what I could not give him,

15

children. I felt that I had no voice in what was going on in the house. My husband was very happy when he was with his children. I saw how his face would light up when they came into the room. I loved my husband and I wanted him to be happy. That was all that I thought about, my husband's happiness. That was the most important thing in my life at this time.

Irene: How did you treat Peninnah's children?

Hannah: I treated them with kindness. I wanted them to know that I loved them. I wanted them to be happy. Sometimes, like any child, they would take advantage of me, but this did not bother me. They were only children, and they were only imitating their mother. I did notice that they were nice to me when their father was around. In his presence, we were like one big happy family.

Kent: What advice do you have for us today?

Hannah: There are several things that I would like you to remember.

- God hears and answers prayer. The answers might not be what we want to hear, and sometimes it may even be a No when we want it to be a Yes. You must be willing to accept God's answers, because He knows what is best for you. It can be hard to accept an answer that you don't want to hear. (Do not be anxious about anything, but in everything, by prayer and petition, with thanksgiving, present your request to God. Philippians 4:6 NIV)

- There are times when you might struggle within yourself. You may feel inadequate or over qualified to tackle a task that needs to be done. Don't let that stop you. If you see that no one is going to do the task, you get up and do it. This is the time to pray and ask God for guidance. Be sure that you follow God's instructions without questions. (I must work the works of him that sent me, while it is day; the night cometh, when no man can work. John 9:4 KJV)

- Our faith and prayer show us that all we have and receive is on loan from God. I might have had an excuse for being a possessive mother after God answered my prayer, especially since it took me so long to have a baby. But I kept my vow. As difficult as it sounds, one of the greatest joys in having a child is to give that child fully and freely back to God. I entered motherhood prepared to do what all mothers must eventually do, to let go of their children. I tried to be fervent in worship, effective in prayer, and willing to follow through on a very costly commitment. God blessed me further with three other sons and two daughters. And Samuel became Israel's greatest judge. (Devote yourself to prayer, keeping alert in it with an attitude of thanksgiving. Colossians 4:2 NAS)

- We become so worried about having and/or getting the thing we want, that we forget about praying. This is a time that we should pray and ask God for guidance. It is time to show God how much we appreciate all of the things that He has done for us. Thank Him for what He is doing for us right now. Thank Him for your life. Be thankful for every little thing. Show God how much you appreciate Him by not complaining and by waiting patiently on His answer. (Yet those who wait for the Lord will gain new strength; They will mount up with wings like eagles, they shall run and not get tired, they will walk and not become weary. Isaiah 40:31 NAS)

- When you pray, be sure that your motivation is right. God is more likely to say yes to petitions when you surrender your all to Him. Remember that in God, there is joy, unspeakable joy. (But the tax collector stood at a distance. He would not even look up to heaven, but beat his breast and said, 'God, have mercy on me, a sinner.' "I tell you that this mind, rather than the other, went home justified before God. For everyone who exalts himself will be humbled, and he who humbles himself will be exalted." Luke 18:13-14 NI

DEBORAH

A wise woman with authority

(Judges 4-5)

"Now Deborah, a prophetess, the wife of Lapi-doth, was judging Israel at that time."

Judges 4:4 (NKJV)

The period of judges dates from about 1375 B.C. to 1050 B.C. during which time Israel was a confederacy of tribes. The judges came from different tribes and functioned as military leaders and civil magistrates. The book of Judges was written to show the consequences of disobedience to God.

Deborah was one of history's outstanding women. Her husband was Lapidoth. She lived in Canaan as both a prophetess and a judge from approximately 1230 B.C to 1190 B.C. God gave this woman insight and confidence and placed her in a unique position in the Old Testament, unique in that she was not power hungry, but wanted to serve God in every way. Whenever praise came her way, she gave God all the credit. Deborah was a strong-minded person who was also gifted with superior spiritual, mental, and physical powers. She did not deny or resist her position in the culture as a woman and wife, and never allowed herself to be hindered by it either. As a wife, she was strong-willed and strong-bodied. Deborah was mistress of her own house. In other words, she took care of her husband and the household chores. Her story might remind us of the hardships endured by our own pioneer women in travelling across the country with their husbands to dangerous new territories.

Deborah was able to hear messages from God and to tell the people what God wanted. Because of that close relationship with God, she had a great influence among her people. As the only female ever chosen to hold their high office of judge, she demonstrated her wisdom and gave instruction with intuition as well as inspiration. She was quickly responsive in both word and deed in fulfilling her role as judge, and all of Israel was under her jurisdiction. She set up her office under a palm tree where she administered righteous justice and mercy.

God had a specific task for her to do and, with His help, she was able to deliver the Israelites from captivity. The Israelites were serving idol gods at this time, and God was not pleased. She would talk to the Israelites about their unfaithful spiritual condition and rouse them from their laziness and despair. She was devoted to freeing God's people, while trying to instill in them the desire to free themselves from their bondage. Deborah was a dynamic speaker who knew how to excite those who gathered to hear her words of divine wisdom. She offered them a reason to hope for their freedom. She wanted them to understand that all they had to do was to act like they were not afraid and to go out and fight.

As a warrior, she herself was also a dynamic fighter who was a patriotic and inspired heroine, who was bold and daring on the battlefield. She was determined to free her people with words as well as sword, and rescue them from their cruel foes.

As a leader, Deborah knew how encourage her people in what needed to be done. She would not only tell them, but she would show her concern for them by working with them, showing them how to do it. When there was a misunderstanding, she was there to mediate, making sure that everyone was respected. Deborah could not forget the spiritual condition of her people, so she continually reminded them that God was with them at all times.

She was also referred to as the "Mother of Israel," although she had no children of her own. Deborah was there for her people to offer them comfort and understanding. Her highest adornment was her trust in God. She had a heart filled with compassion and love. Her career was brilliant because she served God in every way possible. God gave her the peace and wisdom to lead her people, so she had a song on her lips and a sword in her hand when she went into battle.

With these qualities, Deborah went to war against the Canaanites. She had a general named Barak who was to help her with the troops. But Barak was not an effective leader. He was afraid to fight, so Deborah had to go into battle with him and tell him what to do. This was a different kind of war, where a woman gave the orders and directed the war. Another woman, by the name of Jael, was the actual heroine because she killed Sisera, the leader of the enemy camp. With God's help, these two women, Jael and Deborah, won the battle. After it was over, Deborah and Barak began to sing a song of victory that they had both composed.

Wise women were very rare at this time, but Deborah had something that many men did not have. She had a remarkable relationship with God. Her story shows that God can accomplish great things through anyone who is willing to be led by Him. He has always kept His part of the contract between Himself and Israel. God will always go a step further to prove His eternal love.

If you had the opportunity to ask Deborah a question, what would you ask?

QUESTIONS:

Kellie: Why do you think that the Lord chose you instead of another man for the position of judge?

Deborah: I can't tell you exactly why, but know that God always knows what He is doing. He probably looked around and could not find a man who had my qualities. You see, there are so many people who look on the outside of a person, but God looks at the heart. I did not have what many women had in those days, children. According to the law at that time, I was cursed because I was barren. Now a man would have probably said that I had no business being considered for   the position, being cursed. But God said, "Not so." He saw in me what I did not even see in myself. I had something to prove to myself as well as to others. With God's help, I emerged victorious.

Kent: With many battles going on around the world, why did you have to show Barak what to do? After all, it is the men who claim to know more about the strategies of war.

Deborah: I can't speak for Barak. I know that when I told him it was time to fight, he was very hesitant. I knew that he knew about strategies, because he was a soldier, after all. I think that there are some times in our lives when we look at the situation, and the magnitude of it seems so great that we become afraid. Soldiers are not supposed to show their fear, but sometimes they are afraid, and they make big mistakes and have to live with these mistakes the rest of their lives. Maybe Barak did not want to make a mistake. He knew my position and knew of my reputation. He also knew that I had a deep faith in God and knew that He would make everything all right. He looked up to me. It is hard for many men to admit that they look up to a woman, because they feel that this makes them less of a man. I believe that I demonstrated to Barak that I was not afraid to go with him into battle, because I had confidence in the God that I served. That's all it takes, a willingness to do the will of God and to do it with confidence.

Irene: I noticed that, according to scripture, you gave God the praise for your victory through song. Why?

Deborah: Music and singing has been a part of Israel's culture for many years. The victory song that I sang was written by both Barak and me. We both sang it together. The words were put to music and we had a joyous celebration. This song proclaimed God's credit for the victory in the war. It was an excellent way to preserve and retell my story for generations to come. It makes me appreciate over and over again the goodness of God. Also, when I find myself feeling a little under the weather or feeling sorry for myself, I begin to sing and remember what God is doing for me now, and what He has done for me down through the years. You can do the same thing today. Just think about the goodness of God, then let God put a song in your heart, which He will do. Sing this song joyfully, giving praise to God, and your burdens will become a little lighter. The situation does not change, but your attitude toward the situation changes. You find yourself more content and more willing to wait on guidance from the Lord.

Irene: What was the purpose of the song?

Deborah: The purposes were both religious and political. They were:

- To thank God for the victory over the Canaanites and the deliverance of Israel from defeat and oppression for twenty years
- To celebrate the zeal and bravery of the rulers and the people of certain tribes who had faith in God and volunteered their services against a common foe
- To censure the disbelief and weakened faith of certain tribes who stayed at home, and who needed to return to their covenant with the true God
- To honor God for His supernatural part in the uneven struggle between our two earthly foes
- To curse those who did not refuse to take part in the spoil after the victory was assured

- To bless the woman who was bold enough to slay Sisera
- To show the disappointment and anguish of the mother of Sisera
- To pronounce the blessing upon the people of God and a curse upon their enemies.

Alice: I want to be an executive in a large company one of these days because I know I have the ability to do that type of work. I am hesitant because so many have said that a woman executive usually loses her femininity. In your position as judge, did you ever feel that you had lost your femininity?

Deborah: No, never! I was a wife to my husband and the mistress of my house. When people would come into my home, they found it full of feminine ideas. These were my ideas. This was my work. I kept my house clean, cooked my husband's meals, kept his clothes clean, and kept him company. I did not challenge or exert power over him. You have to know how to separate your work from your home life. In my position as a judge, I had to show that I was the leader. I did this with integrity and compassion. I earned the trust of the people and was able to listen and accept what was being said, even when I disagreed with it. I was also flexible enough to accept change, and I knew when to be authoritative and when to compromise. I knew my place both in the home and on the job. Yes, you can be an executive and yet be feminine. Just remember who you really are and go from there.

Maria: I know there are many men who feel inferior being married to a strong woman. Many of them are called "hen-pecked." Did your husband, Lapidoth, give you any indication that he envied you because of your position?

Deborah: No, my husband knew that God had given me the

ability to do the job that I had to do, and he was quite comfortable with it. I know there were times when he felt intimidated because the people, especially the men, would come to me for advice. I could sense it in his attitude, but this is natural. How many husbands want other men talking to their wives all the time? I would feel that way if, every time I looked around, women were in my husband's face. But we had a secure relationship and trusted each other. We also had a deep faith in God, and this took us through many hardships and misunderstandings.

Kent: You mean to tell me that Lapidoth did not feel a little put-out with all the men around you? After all, with the responsibility that you had as a judge, much of your time was taken away from your marriage. There were no children involved, so that all you had were each other. I know I would feel a little lost if every time I looked up, there was someone there with a problem or concern that needed my wife's attention.

Deborah: Remember what I told Alice. You have to know when to separate your work from your job. When I sat under the palm tree, it was there that I did my job, but when I was at home, it was there that I took care of my marriage. There were times of emergency when I had to deal with the job, and my husband was there to back me up. Consider the time in which I was living. We were being oppressed by the Canaanites, and this was our chance to be released from them. This affected not only the people of Israel, but my husband and myself. But as long as there is love and trust in your marriage, and you are secure in who and what you are, with God's help you can and will make it.

John: Deborah, what advice could you give the man today who is in a relationship with a strong woman?

Alice: I was going to ask a similar question, but I was going to turn it around a little and ask for advice for a woman who is in a relationship with a weak man.

Deborah: Possibilities of conflicts can arise in any relationship, and they can arise from the following:

- Either or both partners not being aware of who they really are
1. One partner's position requiring a lot of time
2. One partner being more outgoing than the other
3. One partner enjoying being with people, and the other wanting more of his or her time
4. One partner making more money or being more successful than the other
5. One partner being more materialistic than the other
6. One partner trying to control the other partner's life
7. Basing their relationship on looks or a certain standing in society
8. One partner being jealous of the other
9. Partners not wanting the same things in life (i.e., house, children, etc.)

(Hot tempers start fights; a calm, cool spirit keeps the peace. The empty-headed treat life as a plaything; the perceptive grasp its meaning and make a go of it. Proverbs 15:18, 21 The Message)

- The best advice that I could offer in any relationship, is:
1. Be sure that God is first in both of your lives
2. Be sure that you love and trust each other
3. Be sure that you are friends
4. Be sure that you are secure in the knowledge of who and what you are
5. Be sure that you enjoy quality time together (and that you have some things in common)
6. Be sure that you are accepting of each other's position in life

7. Be sure that you accept each other's friends and relatives
8. Be sure that you have an open line of communication
9. Be sure that you value each other as well as yourself

   (Live in harmony with one another. Do not be proud, but be willing to associate with people of low position. Do not be conceited. Romans 12:16 NIV)

• My husband and I found out that as long as we acknowledged God in all our ways, everything worked out just fine. It might not have been like we thought it should be, but it was according to the will of God. There are going to be misunderstandings. This is human nature. That is why we are individuals and, as individuals, we are different and deal with things differently. These differences can be either positive or negative, depending on how we individually look at them. (Now the body is not made up of one part but many. If the foot should say, "Because I am not a hand, I do not belong to the body," it would not for that reason cease to be part of the body. And if the ear should say, "Because I am not an eye, I do not belong to the body," it would not for that reason cease to be part of the body. If the whole body was an eye, where would the sense of hearing be? If the whole body was an ear, where would the sense of smell be? But the fact God has arranged the parts in the body, every one of them, just as he wanted them to be. If they were all one part, where would the body be? As it is, there are many parts, but one body. But God has combined the members of the body and has given greater honor to the parts that lacked it, so that there should be no division in the body, but that its parts should have equal concern for each other. If one part suffers, every part suffers with it; if one part is honored, every part rejoices with it. I Corinthian 14:15-20, 24-26 NIV)

- There are many women who have the ability to be an authority over others, including men. You do not have to lose your femininity to do this. You have to know who you are, what you are doing, and the people who are under your authority. You must demonstrate good leadership skills, show that you are trustworthy, and demonstrate a compassionate and respectful nature. You must also know when to be strong and not be afraid to show this side of your nature. A woman needs to learn how to separate her career from her home life, and keep them that way. She needs to take care of her marriage and enjoy doing it. Above all, put God first in your lives, asking Him for guidance. He will show you the right way. (For by grace [unmerited favor of God] given to me I warn everyone among you not to estimate and think of himself more highly than he ought [not to have an exaggerated opinion of his own importance], but to rate his ability with sober judgment, each according to the degree of faith apportioned by God to him. Romans 12:3 Amplified)
- The man should be willing to accept the woman for who she is. He needs to know that being with a strong woman does not make him less of a man. It can enhance him if he knows who and what he is and is secure with this knowledge. He also should be in a position that he himself enjoys. He must love and trust his wife, demonstrating this in everything that he does with her. He should be there for her, communicating with her, growing with her, and making sure that each of them has space and time alone when needed. Again, God must be uppermost in their lives. Finally, to each of you, always remember that God can accomplish great things through people who are willing to be led by Him. (So then we pursue the things which make for peace and the building up of one another. Romans 14:19 NAS)
-

ESTHER

The woman who saved her nation from genocide

(Esther 1-9)

*"Go, gather all the Jews who are present in Shushan, and
fast for me; neither eat nor drink for three days, night or day.
My maids and I will fast likewise. And so I will go in to the
king, which is against the law; and if I perish, I perish."*

Esther 4:16 (NKJV)

The book of Esther is an example of God's divine guidance
and care over our lives. God's sovereignty and power are seen
throughout this book.

The events of Esther span a decade during the reign of the
Persian King, Xerxes I (486–465 B.C.). He had a wife and queen
named Vashti who refused to do his bidding, so he had her banished.
He was an absolute ruler, erratic decision maker, brutal in some
cases, unpredictable and inaccessible.

The search for a new queen began. A decree was sent out to
gather together all the beautiful women in the empire and take
them to the royal harem. Esther, whose Jewish name was Hadasah,
was one of the Hebrew captives in the Persian state of the tribe of
Benjamin. The Jews were the minority since their deportation from
Judan 100 years earlier, and the Persians were hostile to them. She

was an orphan who had been raised by her cousin Mordecai. Esther was beautiful. She is presented as a woman of piety, faith, courage, heroism, and resourcefulness.

Esther was one of the many beautiful women who were chosen to be a part of King Xerxes' harem. She had great personal beauty with dark exotic features, physical charms, and a personality and character which enhanced her beauty and gave it distinction. It was customary for the virgins in the king's harem to spend a year in beauty treatments and purification rites before going to see the king. Beautiful young virgins were to exist merely to bring pleasure to the kings. After the year passed, the virgins were brought before the king, and he had the opportunity to pick the one that he liked best. He chose Esther because of her beauty, and she became queen.

Esther's cousin, Mordecai, had an official position within the king's gate where important business took place. A Persian by the name of Haman was promoted to the position of chief minister by the king. He wanted all the recognition and honor. He expected everyone to show him homage, but Mordecai refused to do so. Haman resented Mordecai, so he proposed the destruction of all the Jews. He even persuaded the king to pass a decree to exterminate the Jews. A royal decree went out all over the land that all of the Jewish people were to be killed.

Mordecai recognized the threat to his people, so he told Esther that she had to do something about it. Esther understood that Mordecai was asking her to risk her life. She was very fearful. She had not been summoned by the king for thirty days. But she agreed to intervene with the king on behalf of her people. Along with all the Jewish people, she fasted and prayed for three days. She knew that she would be breaking the law, and that she could die with her people by approaching the king before being summoned. After the fast, she approached the king and he was happy to see her. She asked that a small banquet be prepared and that Haman should also be invited. Haman was excited and honored to think that the queen would invite only him to a banquet, not once, but twice.

During the banquet, Esther was able to expose Haman as the culprit who was going to destroy Mordecai. Haman became terrified.

The king was so angry that he walked out of the room. Haman began to beg Esther for leniency and fell on her couch. When the king walked in, he found Haman in that compromising position. The king became outraged and covered Haman's head, which meant that he was going to die. Haman was condemned to die on the same gallows that he had built for Mordecai. Queen Esther and the Jewish people were saved.

Can you think of any questions that you would like to ask Esther?

QUESTIONS:

Alice: You had heard about the decree from the king about the search for beautiful women. How did you feel when Mordecai approached you and told you that you were going to be one of the women who would go before the king?

Esther: At first I did not like the idea, but I trusted Mordecai and knew that he would not do anything to hurt me. I did not want to leave him, but he told me that I had to, so I did. I did not believe that I would be chosen because I didn't think that I would be considered pretty enough.

Kent: Did you ever think to question Mordecai about his decision to involve you in the king's contest?

Esther: No, I felt that since he had raised me, he knew what was best for me. You see, I had enough faith in Mordecai to believe that he would not do anything to cause me harm. I have to admit though that I did wonder why he felt that I was pretty enough even to participate in the contest. I did not see myself as pretty. I was just an ordinary person doing what I needed to do to get by.

Maria: How did you feel when you were actually chosen to be one of the women?

Esther: I felt scared and honored. I was afraid because I did not know what was really going to happen. I knew that I had to leave my home and Mordecai, but since he had reassured me that everything would be alright, I was content. I was honored though, because I did not think that I'd be chosen.

John: Just think, you were a participant in the first beauty contest in the world! How did this make you feel with all the other beautiful women surrounding you? I'm sure there must have been some kind of friction because of the high level of competition.

Esther: Yes, there was friction. The women were comparing themselves to each other, each claiming to be more beautiful than the other. We were getting a lot of nice attention, considering the difference in our backgrounds. None of us wanted to return to our impoverished homes. I have to admit that I also enjoyed all the attention that we were getting. It also seemed that I was getting a little more attention than the rest of the girls, and this did go to my head for a little while. I had to talk to myself many times to keep from becoming proud.

Irene: What did you think about your future husband, King Xerxes?

Esther: I had only seen him at a distance. He was not a bad looking man. I was a little afraid of him because I had heard that he had banished his first wife, Queen Vashti. I did not understand the reason behind the banishment, but who am I to question? The king was a powerful man, and he could do whatever he wanted to. I think the thing that affected me most was whether or not the king would like me for the person I was. I was to be chosen for my beauty, nothing else. There were many questions that were running through my mind. What did he know about me? What did I really know about him? What if he didn't like me? What if I could not please him? What if I did not know how to act in public? What if, what if, what if? So, you see, I had many concerns, but mostly about myself. I had no say as to who my husband was to be anyway. I was chosen by him, so I had to accept the inevitable. To put it bluntly though, I was just plain scared.

Kellie: After your marriage, was it hard for you to adjust to a totally different lifestyle? After all, you came from poverty and moved into royalty.

Esther: It was very hard. I had to get used to being waited on. As I was growing up, I did all my own house work, including the cooking and cleaning. I took care of my own private needs. If I wanted to take a walk, I would do so. This was not so in the palace. Everything that I needed was provided for me. If I wanted anything, all I had to do was say so. I had servants and I gave them orders. There was always someone with me, wherever I went in the palace. There was no privacy. I had my own side of the palace with the other women. The men, on the other hand, were with the king. Sometimes I felt like I was in prison. But above everything else, I only saw my husband when he sent for me. There were times when I felt that I wanted to see him, but I could not because I had not been sent for. This was not like any marriage that I knew of. There were many times when I would be lonely, even when I was surrounded by people. They did not know that I was Jewish, so there were many things that I could not talk about. It was an easy life, as far as material things go, but emotionally it was hard.

Alice: Why was it hard when you had everything that you wanted?

Esther: Material things are just not enough. You cannot appreciate what a real life is all about if there are no hardships and nothing materially lacking. Riches are not everything. In order to have a full life, you need more than what money can buy. You have to know that you are loved and needed. You need to know that you are accepted for yourself. You should feel that you can make mistakes and learn from them without being criticized. You especially need to know who you are, and be willing to accept yourself for being the person that you really are. These are the things that I missed.

John: When you got word from Mordecai about Haman's plans for the Jewish people, what was your first reaction? After all, you are also a Jew.

Esther: My first reaction was that this could not be happening to me. Here I am the queen, and Haman was trying to destroy my people. Then I stopped to think a minute, and I remembered that no one knew I was Jewish. Mordecai had told me to keep that information to myself. I did not understand at first, but then I began to understand his reasoning. My second thought was how can I help my people? What could I, the queen, do without ruining myself? Then I thought of Mordecai. He was all the family that I had. I could not go on living knowing that I had done nothing to help him. I remembered my God. It was time for me to pray.

John: When did you decide to take action?

Esther: When I remembered to pray. There is something about prayer. When I prayed to God, I felt a sense of relief. It was as if He were directing me in the steps that I needed to take. Remember, I believed in prayer and fasting. I believed that God would help us if we would just do something together, in unity. I sent word to Mordecai to get all the Jewish people together for three days of fasting and praying. It was amazing the way all of the people cooperated. I knew that I needed to do the same thing. I also prayed and fasted, asking God for directions. The Jewish people did not know whether I could do anything, but they had the faith to believe that God was able to make everything turn out all right. I too had to believe.

Alice: Were you afraid when you approached the king without him sending for you?

Esther: I was terrified. I kept thinking, what if he would not see me? What if he gave me permission to approach him and then changed his mind? What if he did see me, but would not allow me to do what I had in mind? Yet in the back of my mind, I recognized that I could not allow my feelings to stop me from doing what I knew was necessary.

Maria: I know you were trying to get the king to see Haman for what he really was, but why did you have to have two banquets?

Esther: I wanted Haman to feel comfortable in my presence. I knew he thought a lot of himself because of what I had heard about him. I did not realize that the king, in the meantime, would remember all that Mordecai had done for him in the past and had never been properly rewarded. My own plans were almost ruined when Haman was told to honor Mordecai. So the necessity of having another banquet planned became important. Haman was beside himself. The idea that he had to honor Mordecai was against his better judgment. But he remembered that he himself was still invited to another banquet with the king and queen, and this was very important to him. This was something to look forward to. Even though he was disgusted at having to honor Mordecai, Haman was able to rise above it with the knowledge that he would see the king and queen again.

Maria: What do you think Haman was thinking when he arrived at the second banquet?

Esther: He probably thought that everything was status quo. Here he was again in the presence of the king and queen. Here he was the only one invited to the banquet again. Here he could enjoy the honor he deserved. He was in seventh heaven. He was not expecting to hear anything negative about himself.

John: What happened when you accused Haman of trying to destroy the Jewish nation?

Esther: After my accusations, you should have seen his face. He was in shock. He did not know what was going to happen next. He was having such a good time, you see, and then I had to ruin it. When the king was so angry that he walked out of the room, this was just too much for Haman. He began to beg me to change my mind. He was so overwrought that he had lost control of himself. When I would not relent, he literally fell onto the couch where I was sitting. I don't think he did it on purpose; it was just such a shattering situation. He did not know how to get me to change my mind. When the king walked back into the room and saw him on my couch, the king was outraged. He covered Haman's face and called for his servants. Haman knew what this meant and he began to cry in fear. It was a very emotional time.

Kent: What did the covering of the head mean?

Esther: The covering was placed over his head because he was found in such a compromising position, lying on the queen's couch. When the king returned and saw the situation, he became angrier. Haman's head was covered because no one was to look at him again. Anyone that was involved in such a shameful situation lost all rights to either look at another or to be looked upon by others. At that moment, he was condemned to die. The most ironic part of this whole situation was that he was hanged on the same gallows that he had built for Mordecai.

Alice: After Haman's death, what was your life like?

Esther: I settled into my life as the queen and was very content. My people were free and doing very well. Mordecai was where I was able to talk with him when I needed to. I had a son that I loved. My husband sent for me more frequently, and this really pleased me.

Irene: Do you have any advice for us today?

Esther: Yes I have.

- Today, I believe that a lot of emphasis is being placed on what the media considers as beauty. You have to be a certain size, have a certain shape, a certain look, and wear certain types of clothing. I believe this applies to both the men and the women. Another thing, many people use their beauty to exploit or to take advantage of a situation. But remember, physical beauty is only skin deep. Don't base everything you do on your looks. It's what's inside a person that's important. There are many people who are not very pretty according to society's standards, but who demonstrate a beautiful attitude. This includes compassion, tenderness, empathy, friendliness, good morals, and honesty. When you find such a person, you find beauty. These things are very important, but when one uses his or her beauty to do the will of the Lord, this is much more important. You are willing to make the sacrifices for the good of others. You don't mind getting dirty, wearing less make-up, and even wearing old clothing in order to reach out and help others. This is what real beauty is all about. (And whatever you do, whether in word or deed, do it all in the name of the Lord Jesus, giving thanks to God the Father through him. Colossians 3:17 NIV)

- Another important thing is to respect your parents or guardians, no matter what your age is, or how wrong you think they are. They are the ones who have gone through many things to nurture and educate you. There have been hardships, I'm sure. But through these hardships, your parents/guardians stuck by your side, demonstrating their love for you. Mordecai stayed close to me, even though my economic status had changed. I never thought that I was too good for him and vice versa. As young people you are expected to do a little better than your parents/guardians in many cases. Don't forget your roots. Don't forget from where you came. Don't forget your heritage. (Children, do what your parents tell you. This delights the Master no end. Parents don't come down too hard on your children or you'll crush their spirits. Colossians 3:20-21 The Message)
- Opportunities may come along that are more important for you than other opportunities that seem more appealing. Be sure to appreciate those important opportunities and take advantage of them. You never know when another such chance will happen again. As the queen, such an opportunity happened for me. When my people, the Jews, were being abused, I had the opportunity to save them. It was a hard decision that I had to make, but I made it. I knew that if I failed, it would cost me my life, as well as the lives of my people. I had to take that chance, and I have never regretted it to this day. Be sure to trust God to put together events in your life that will benefit you, even if you cannot see the overall picture. Ask God for guidance in everything that you do, and He will show you the way. Obey God's directions. If you follow them, things will work out all right. (In all your ways acknowledge him, and he will make your paths straight. Proverbs 3:8 NIV)

- Prejudice is not good. It grows out of personal pride or a quest for power. When you begin to consider yourself better than others, hatred and prejudice can set in. People who do this are selfish and want things to go their way all of the time. Consider Haman, he let power go to his head because of his prejudice and hatred for the Jewish nation. Look where he ended up, hanging on the gallows that he had built for someone else. (Pride goeth before destruction and a haughty spirit before a fall. Proverbs 16:18 KJV)

- Try to get your priorities straight. Examine the pros and cons. Determine a course of action and move ahead. Don't always try to find the easiest way out. Don't lessen your commitment only to what you know you are capable of doing. Don't procrastinate. The old proverb, "Don't put off 'til tomorrow what you can do today," is very practical in all situations. Keep it in mind the next time you decide to let a golden opportunity pass you by. There are times when you have to do something that is not popular with the majority. You might think that you are alone in the decisions that you feel you have to make. If you feel that it is the right thing to do, do it. It may not make you popular and you may have to change the way you do things. You don't have to understand the need or the reasons for these changes, but remember that God is still in control. (Only do not rebel against the Lord. And do not be afraid of the people of the land, because we will swallow them up. Their protection is gone, but the Lord is with us. Do not be afraid of them. Numbers 14:9 NIV)

MIRIAM

The woman whose jealousy brought judgment

(Exodus 15:20-21; Numbers 12:1-15; 20:1; 26:59)

"And Miriam answered them, Sing ye to the Lord,
for He has triumphed gloriously; the horse and
his rider hath he thrown into the sea."

Exodus 15:21 (KJV)

Miriam was the sister of Moses, the prophet who led the children of Israel out of the land of Egypt across the Red Sea to freedom.

When Miriam, an Israelite, was about twelve years old, she and her family lived in Egypt as slaves. Pharaoh signed a decree that all the boys born to the Israelites were to be killed. This was done because they were multiplying too fast. You see, the Israelites were the slaves of the Egyptians. Miriam's mother was pregnant at the time and, when her time came, she had a boy. She kept him hidden for three months. But the time came when she could no longer hide him. She did not want him to die so she made a basket to hide him, and she placed the basket into a river.

Miriam was told to stand by the river and watch the basket. At that time the daughter of Pharaoh decided to bathe in the river. When she saw the basket, she sent one of her maids to get it out of the water. When the basket was brought to her, she saw the baby in it. The baby, Moses, began to cry, and the princess had compassion on it. Miriam was hiding in the bushes, but when she saw that she was not going to kill Moses, she asked if she could get a nurse to care for him. The princess gave her permission to do so, and Miriam went and got her mother. Her mother was told to take and nurse the baby and, when he was weaned, he was to be taken to the palace to live with the princess.

Miriam did not get to see her brother Moses again, until he returned to Egypt as a grown married man. He had come back to free the Israelites from the Egyptians. When Pharaoh let them go, Miriam was a part of the Israelite group that walked away from Egypt to freedom. When they got to the Red Sea, there was no way to cross to the other side. Pharaoh's army was behind them and the Red Sea was in front of them. God provided a way across the Red Sea for the Israelites. He told Moses to stretch out the rod that he had in his hand over the Red Sea, and He would divide the waters so that the Israelites could cross over on dry land. After they had crossed, Moses again stretched out his hand, the Red Sea came together again, and the Egyptians were drowned. When the Israelites saw what God had done for them and knew they were safe, Miriam took out a tambourine and led the women in a dance of victory. They were so excited that they were no longer slaves.

They were on their way to the Promised Land. Miriam gradually became jealous of the prestige given her brother Moses, and spoke out against him. She could not accept the fact that God only spoke to Moses. She thought that she was just as good as Moses. God did speak to her and gave her to understand that He alone was the one who made the prophets. God was very angry with her, and she became afflicted with leprosy. In those days, anyone with leprosy could not live among the people because this disease was very contagious. Miriam was quarantined for seven days until God healed her. She felt blessed because many people died of this disease. The Israelites did not travel until Miriam was able to go with them.

The Israelites lived by the Red Sea for a while, and also camped in the wilderness. They traveled from place to place for about forty years. At the end of the forty years, during the first month after the

Israelites arrived at the desert of Zin, Miriam died. She never got to see the Promised Land.

What questions would you like to ask Miriam?

QUESTIONS:

Kellie: How did you feel when your mother had to give up your little brother?

Miriam: I did not like it at all. I was the one who helped take care of him, and I really loved him. He was very special to me. I cried when the Egyptians came and took him away. My mother tried to comfort me, but I could not be comforted.

Irene: Why is it that you never married?

Miriam: I don't believe it was in God's plan for me to marry and have children. There was never any man who showed any interest in me. In my day, the man had to approach the woman and/or the woman's family. No one ever did this for me.

Irene: Were you content with your life as a slave?

Miriam: No, I was not content. I did what I had to do, but I was also praying and hoping that someday I would be free. I prayed to God that He would send someone to rescue us, and deliver us from Egypt.

Maria: How did you feel when you saw your brother again, after all the years of separation?

Miriam: I guess you can say that I was of two minds. I was glad to see him alive and well, but I was afraid for him because of what he said he had to do.

John: How did you feel when you found out that God had chosen your brother to go to Pharaoh to ask him for the release of the Israelites?

Miriam: I was in awe to think that my brother had returned to deliver us from bondage. After all, I hadn't seen him in about forty years. I hadn't heard from him. I knew nothing about him, and I didn't know where he had been. He was a stranger to me, and for him to come back and go to Pharaoh was awesome. It was a wonderful feeling. After all, he was my brother!

John: Were you a prophetess?

Miriam: Yes

John: What is a prophetess?

Miriam: A prophetess is one that is called by God and inspired by His spirit to proclaim the will and purpose of God.

Kent: In that case, what do you think your mission was?

Miriam: I believe my mission was to stand with my brother Moses, and to help him in any way that I could.

Irene: After crossing the Red Sea, why did you play music and dance?

Miriam: I was so happy to be safe, away from the Egyptians that I just had to do something. I picked up my tambourine and danced around with it, beating it to keep my rhythm. I was giving praise to God. I was thanking Him for helping us to safety without having to fight. I was also thanking Him for our being freed from bondage. There were no casualties. The other women joined me in my praise, and we had a great time together.

Alice: Why were you jealous of Moses?

Miriam: I was jealous because of all the attention he was getting from the people. It was as if he could do no wrong. Anything that he told the people to do, they would do it. They would follow blindly behind him. They did not seem to be able to do anything without first getting his

permission. I admit that I wanted some of that attention. In fact, I needed some of that prestige. I wanted the
people to look up to me, and I wanted to be admired.
Simply put, I wanted what Moses had.

Maria: Could you have been jealous because you were a prophetess?

Miriam: Well, yes, it could have been. After all, there were
times in my life that God had spoken to me directly. He
was no longer talking to me since Moses had come back.
I would pray and ask God why He was no longer talking
to me, but I would not get an answer. This really troubled me. It seemed that all of my prayers were useless. I
guess you can say that this was another reason why I was
so jealous of my brother.

Kellie: You were so jealous that you tried to turn the people against Moses?

Miriam: Yes, I went a little too far. Moses was such a humble
man that the people loved him. They did not like what
I was trying to do. More importantly, God did not like
what I was trying to do, so He punished me. I became
afflicted with leprosy.

Kent: What is leprosy?

Miriam: Leprosy is a very contagious disease. People who had it
developed sores all over their body. There was no cure for
it. In its advanced stage, people could start losing parts of
their limbs. When people found out that you had leprosy, you could no longer live with the town people. You
had to go and live among other lepers.

Alice: How did you feel about the leprosy?

Miriam: Now that's a silly question. No one wants to be sick,
especially with leprosy. It was a very dangerous disease.
I knew I was being punished by God. I was sick. I was

ashamed. I was humiliated. I was an outcast. I could no longer live among the people. I was the very opposite of what I really wanted to be. There was no respect. No one looked up to me, and no one wanted to be around me. It was terrible.

Kellie: How did you feel when you were healed?

Miriam: I felt relieved and wonderful. God had forgiven me because He had healed me from an incurable disease. Not only had He healed me, but He had not allowed me to suffer for the many years that others with the disease suffer. I was praising and thanking God for giving me another chance to serve Him. I had achieved now another type of freedom, freedom from disease and freedom from jealousy.

Kent: How did you feel about your brother not moving the camp until you could go with them?

Miriam: I was very grateful for this. This also reassured me that God was with him, and approved the way that Moses was working with the people.

Maria: What advice do you have for us?

Miriam:

- Be sure that you use the gifts, talents, and skills that God has given you. If you are good at sports, play them. If you are good in academics, stick to them. Don't let anyone tease you or make you feel bad because you are an A student. (For this reason I remind you to kindle afresh the gift of God which is in you through the laying on of the hands. For God has not given us the spirit of timidity, but of power and love and discipline. II Timothy 1:6-7 NAS)
- Don't be jealous of anyone else who you feel is more popular than you are, or because he has a gift that you

would like to have. It does not take popularity to be special. Everyone is special in some way. (For where jealousy and selfish ambition exist, there is disorder and every evil thing. James 3:16 NAS)

- It takes ordinary people to do God's will. Remember that God uses ordinary people who are willing to do what He asks them to do. He does not want a lot of excuses; instead He wants a willing and obedient person. He is not looking for scholars or popularity; He is only looking for willingness. Pray and ask God to direct you in all of your daily activities. (In all your ways acknowledge Him, And He will make your paths straight. Proverbs 3:6 NIV)

- Accept your calling from the Lord. Whatever God has planned for you, accept it and He will direct and bless you. Be the best that you can be. In whatever you do, do your best. It does not matter how small the task may seem, just do your best. You will get satisfaction from doing it, and the person for whom it is being done will also get some satisfaction and thank you. (The Lord came and stood there, calling as the other times, "Samuel, Samuel!" Then Samuel said "Speak Lord, for your servant is listening." I Samuel 310 NIV)

- Learn all you can about yourself. No one should know you better than yourself. You know your own short comings. You know what you can and cannot do. Stand for right and don't let anyone lead you wrong. Set goals for yourself. Strive to reach those goals. There will be some failures, but they should not stop you from trying to reach your goals. Upon accomplishing each goal, set another. Keep setting them and working toward each of them. Be happy with who you are. (Only let us live up to what we have already attained. Philippians 3:16 NIV)

JEZEBEL

Not exalted (A she-devil)

(1 King 16:31; 18:4-19; 19:1-2; 21:5-25, 2 Kings 9)

*"And the dogs shall eat Jezebel in the portion of Jez-
reel, and there shall be none to bury her."*

2 Kings 9:10 (KJV)

Jezebel was a Phoenician princess, the daughter of King Ithobaal
I of Tyre. The Phoenicians worshipped Baal, and Jezebel was
also a Baal priestess. She was very beautiful and had been told so
from her childhood. She also knew how to use her beauty to her
advantage.

Jezebel was so beautiful that King Ahab of the Israelites married
her, and she became queen. She had so much control over Ahab that
she was able to get everything she wanted. She even convinced him
to build a temple in honor of Baal, a pagan god, even though it was
against his religion. You see, the Israelites believed in the true and
living God and were never supposed to worship idols.

Jezebel ordered that everyone should worship her god, Baal.
The king himself was so influenced by Jezebel that he issued a royal
decree regarding the worship of Baal, and thus led the Israelites into
sin. All of the prophets of God then were killed or went into hiding.

One prophet by the name of Elijah, however, would not give in to her orders. He was determined to continue prophesying and teaching about his God. He even challenged Baal to a duel to determine which god was living and true and the most powerful. Jezebel was devastated when Elijah won.

After this, many of the Israelites returned to serving God. This really upset Jezebel, and she lost some of her following. She continued trying to influence King Ahab and every other important man that she thought could help her cause.

Elijah had prophesied that the dogs would lick up the blood of Ahab. King Ahab became more afraid because he remembered Elijah's prophecy about his death. His people were at war, so he decided to participate. He disguised himself as a regular soldier and gave his royal garments to another soldier. That soldier was killed and so was Ahab. The dogs licked up his blood as Elijah had prophesied. Ahab's son Ahaziah became king. He was just a figurehead because he did whatever Jezebel told him to do. He was also killed in the war. Another one of Jezebel's sons became king, and he also was only a figurehead and ultimately killed.

Jehu, a man she could not control, became king. Jezebel tried and tried to entice him, to no avail. He ordered his servants to kill her by throwing her out of the window. Elijah's prophecy that she was to be eaten by dogs was being fulfilled. No one picked her up, and the dogs consumed every part of her body, except for her skull, feet, and hands.

What questions would you like to ask Jezebel?

QUESTIONS:

Kellie: Did you consider Baal to be a keeper and guide?

Jezebel: We were taught that Baal's prophets could talk with him and they, in turn, would respond to his people. We, as a people, were very loyal.

John: You did not think that those prophets were taking advantage of you?

Jezebel: No, I did not. You see, I was trained from a child that Baal was my god, and that I had to follow his rules. When I was told to jump, I did not ask any questions.

Irene: Did rebellion ever enter your mind?

Jezebel: I think we all want to rebel at some time or other in our lives. So, I'm sure that I tried to rebel. You need to remember that I lived a charmed life. I was a princess who got everything that I wanted. I was catered to with servants to do my bidding. Everyone thought I was beautiful. I could take advantage of any and everyone I wanted to, so why would I have to rebel?

Alice: In other words, you were spoiled?

Jezebel: I guess you could say that. Yes, I was spoiled and I took advantage of everything and everyone that I could. I got away with many things.

Maria: I heard that you used makeup to make yourself more beautiful. Who taught you how to use it?

Jezebel: As I said before, I was pampered with a lot of servants. They taught me how to use makeup to my advantage. They showed me how to put it on and how much to use in one setting. They also showed me how to mix it so that I would get the right combination and color. In my day, we did not have all of the advantages that you have today. We had to go through a lot of changes to get what we wanted.

Alice: You were a beautiful woman, so why did you have to use makeup?

Jezebel: When I was introduced to it, I saw how, when it was done right, it enhanced my beauty. I was determined to look better than everyone else. I had set my goals high, and I knew that this was one way to do so. Every since I was a child, everyone would brag about how pretty I was. I got a lot of attention and I enjoyed that attention. When I used makeup, I got the same type of attention, and it was wonderful.

Kent: You said that you learned how to entice men. What did you mean by enticing men?

Jezebel: When I was younger, I got everything I wanted from my father by asking, demanding, pouting, or being angry. As I grew older, I found that I could use these same tactics on other males. I also found that when I added the makeup and flirted a little, I could get my way with most men. I usually would make promises that I had no intention of keeping. I hurt a lot of men that way.

Kent: Did you ever get caught?

Jezebel: Yes, on several occasions. As I said before, I had hurt a lot of men in my lifetime. But being who I was, a princess, and later a queen, I was able to get away with many things. This is what I was used to and what I expected.

Kellie: History has stated that you were a heartless woman with a bloody history. What do you have to say about that?

Jezebel: Well, I was heartless. I wanted everything to go my way, and I did whatever I felt was necessary to get it. I did not like anyone to tell me that I was wrong in anything I did. If they were against me and I found out, I had them killed. I was so selfish in my way of thinking that it was my way or the highway.

Maria: Did you love your husband?

Jezebel: In the beginning, I was in awe of him because he was a king with a large kingdom, and he wanted to marry me. I saw this as an opportunity to better myself. As years passed, I realized that I could manipulate him and get whatever I wanted. So, I suppose you can say that I was never in love with Ahab, I just fell in love with what he represented, and what he could give me.

Irene: Did you feel the same with your sons?

Jezebel: I guess I did. I was a powerful woman and wanted to stay that way. My sons loved me and I took advantage of that love. They wanted to please their mom and I wanted them to please and love me.

John: Was there ever a man you were afraid of?

Jezebel: Yes, there were two that I can remember, Elijah and Jehu. Elijah would not leave me alone. He was always talking about his God and how powerful He was. He kept saying that my god was nothing but a statue. I felt so insulted that I challenged him and his God. Elijah and his God won the duel, and I was devastated. The people lost confidence in Baal and returned to the God of Israel. I even tried to have Elijah killed, but he kept escaping. The other man was Jehu. I tried and tried to seduce him, and I thought I had him under my spell, but I was wrong. Boy was I wrong.

Kellie: Did you ever ask yourself how the men felt when you made fools out of them?

Jezebel: I really did not care as long as I got what I wanted from them.

Kent: During your time as a queen, didn't you ever feel sorry for what you were doing to others?

Jezebel: To be honest with you, I would have to say no. I was too involved with my life, so I really did not take the time to focus on anything else but what I wanted. I guess, in this day, I would probably be classified as a person without a conscience.

Kent: What about your husband? Didn't you feel bad about what you were doing to him?

Jezebel: Not really! He was just someone that I could use. When I found out that I could manipulate him, I just took control and did what I wanted. As long as I was there for him, he was happy. I gave him what he wanted and he seemed to be satisfied. He learned early to stay out of my way. Did I feel bad? No, I felt powerful.

John: What advice could you give us?

Jezebel: Let me see, and I'm not asking you to be like me. But I advise the following:

- Know and respect yourself. Be honest with yourself and don't be selfish. The only way that you can truly be happy is to be willing to accept yourself for who you really are. Then you will be aware of your limitations and your strengths. Being selfish won't get you anywhere. The idea of me, me, me, and no one else, does not benefit you in anyway. The attitude that I don't want to be involved if I'm not the big shot, or count me out if it does not benefit me in some way, is no good and has to go. Do what you can do to the best of your ability. Do something for someone else without expecting any type of reward. This will make you feel good about yourself. (If anyone thinks he is something when he is nothing, he deceives himself. Galatians 6:3 NIV)

- It is time to think of others, respect and be kind to them. Take this time to listen. You will be surprised how much you can learn by just listening. Consider other's advice and suggestions, especially your parents. Show respect, first for yourself and then toward others. You can get more accomplished with kindness and good manners than with dishonesty and bad manners. Reach out to those who are less fortunate than you are. Maybe one of your goals might be: To demonstrate respect in everything that you do. (. . . and let us consider how to stimulate one another to love and do good deeds. Hebrews 10:24 NAS)

- If you just happen to be the best in some situation or activity, keep a level head. Don't lord it over those who are not as good as you are. Be a friend. Don't forget those who have helped you along the way. Who knows, one of these days you might have to call on them again. (Humble yourself in the sight of the Lord, and he shall lift you up. James 4:10 KJV)

- Don't make promises that you don't plan to keep, especially if they are only made to get what you want. A promise should be made with your sincere desire to keep it. Your goal should be that you want to retain the trust that people have in you. If you cannot keep the promise, be sure to let the person know. (When you make a vow to God, do not delay in fulfilling it. He has no pleasure in fools: fulfill your vow. It is better not to vow than to make a vow and not fulfill it. Ecclesiastes 5:4-5 NIV)

- To the girls: Use makeup to enhance your beauty and not to entice others. Be modest and don't overdo it. Also, be sure that your parents have given you permission to wear it. The beauty that shines from within is more powerful. People see that beauty because it is the real you. It is the true beauty that really counts. (Therefore, I urge you, brothers, in view of God's mercy, to offer your bodies as living sacrifices, holy and pleasing to God – thus is your spiritual act of worship. Do not conform any longer to the pattern of this world, but be transformed by the renewing of your mind. Then you will be able to test and approve what God's will is – his good, pleasing and perfect will. Romans 12:1-2 NIV)

VASTI

She exalted modesty

(Esther 1)

"But Queen Vasti refused to come at the king's command brought by his eunuchs; therefore the king was furious, and his anger burned within him."

Esther 1:12 (NKJV)

Vasti was a Persian woman who married King Ahasuerus, the ruler of India and Ethiopia. She was a beautiful woman. She was proud to have been chosen as queen. She had her own apartments in the palace where she entertained the women. She was not allowed to be with the men unless she was summoned by the king.

At one point, King Ahasuerus was having a party which lasted seven days. Apparently, the king had been bragging about Vasti's beauty, and he wanted to show her off to the men. On the seventh day while the royal wine was flowing freely, he sent his servants to get Vasti. According to the servants, he wanted her to appear naked, with only a crown on her head. She refused to go to the king's gathering.

The king was very angry. His counselors suggested that he get rid of Vasti before the other women heard about what she had done.

If he did not do this, the other women would try to do the same thing. Vasti was removed from the palace and never seen or heard from again.

This is not very informative, but what would you ask Vasti if you had the chance?

QUESTIONS:

Irene: Did you feel that you were beautiful?

Vasti: I know I had been told so many times in my short life that I was beautiful. I used to take it with a grain of salt. I accepted the fact that I was unusual. I guess I considered myself pretty.

Alice: Now, come on, you know whether you are pretty or not.

Vasti: You are right, Alice. Every woman knows whether she is pretty. Yes, I was a very pretty woman, but I didn't flaunt it.

John: Did the king marry you because of your looks?

Vasti: Yes, he did. He loved to have beautiful things around him, including women. He searched for a woman with good looks to marry and, when he saw me, he thought that I was a good candidate. Yes, he married me because I was beautiful in his eyes.

Kent: How did you feel knowing this?

Vasti: It didn't bother me at first. I thought that I could change his mind, and that he would get to know the real me and see the type of person I was. This is what I really wanted to happen.

Alice: Why did the men and women have separate quarters?

Vasti: This was the custom in my day. Whenever a party or banquet was given, the men and women were in separate parts of the house. The women were considered to be of less importance than men. They would sometimes serve the men, and then leave them to their celebrations. The women had no say in how the country was being run, the policies that were made, the decisions that affected them, and the laws. They were inferior to men.

Maria: How did that make you feel?

Vasti: It did not bother me. I was used to the role that I had to play in my life. I knew my place and I rather enjoyed it. I enjoyed being with the women. We would get together and talk about many female topics. With so many cultures involved, I learned a lot from each of them. It was a very interesting way of life.

Kent: King Ashauerus celebrated for seven days. Why was it so wrong for the king to send for his queen in order to show her off?

Vasti: It was not wrong for the king to send for me, just unusual. He had never asked for me to appear before his guests naked. He had to be drunk.

John: What's so wrong about a man wanting to show off his wife if she is beautiful?

Vasti: The request was not wrong. The way he wanted me to appear was wrong. Would you want your girl friend to appear before your friends dressed inappropriately or not dressed at all? Would you want all of them to sneer at her and make snide remarks about her? I didn't think so. Well, I did not want to be treated that way either. It was against everything I stood for, and I could not see lowering my standards even for the king.

Irene: You made the king very unhappy when you refused his summons. How did this make you feel?

Vasti: I felt alright because I was doing what I knew was best for me. I realized that I would lose my self-respect if I exposed myself like the king wanted. I knew who I was, and I maintained my dignity.

Maria: Did you think the king would let you get away with it?

Vasti: I thought that I would be able to talk with him and explain myself. When we were alone, we had many serious conversations before. I figured that this would be one of those times when we could have one of those conversations.

Kellie: When his men came for you, what did you think then?

Vasti: I really didn't know what to think. They wouldn't talk to me. I thought they would take me to the king so that I could talk to him. When they did not take me to the king, I was really worried. One of them decided to answer my questions, after I pleaded with them. I had embarrassed the king and, therefore,I was being relieved of my duties as queen.

Maria: What happened to you?

Vasti: While some say that I was banished from the kingdom, and others say that I was beheaded, I preferred the first option. Certainly banishment is more favorable than having my head cut off for not going against my personal standards.

Irene: What advice do you have for us?

Vasti:

- Know yourself. Know your standards. Know what you believe in. Know how you feel about certain things. Stick to your principles. Don't let anyone lead you astray. Stick with what you know is right. Make a stand.

Don't lower your standards for anyone. If you are asked to do something that makes you uncomfortable, don't do it. Example: Why smoke marijuana, if you have never done it before. Who cares what they call you. Let them. It might hurt for a little while, but in the long run it will bother you less and less. Why try to impress someone by taking yourself down. They, in turn, will notice where you are coming from and admire you for being able to take a stand for what you know is right. (So then, brothers, stand firm and hold to the teachings we passed on to you, whether by word of mouth or by letter. 2 Thessalonians 2:15 NIV)

- Hold on to your modesty. You don't have to look or be like everyone else. You know your shape and what looks best on you. If you are a short chubby person, you know that you would not look right in some things that a tall skinny person would wear, and vice versa. Your makeup does not have to make you look like a clown. By learning how to wear the correct amount and the right color combinations, you can enhance your inner beauty. (Also [I desire] that women should adorn themselves modestly and appropriately and sensibly in seemly apparel, not with [elaborate] hair arrangement or gold or pearls or expensive clothing. But by doing good deeds [deeds in themselves good and for the good and advantage of those contacted by them], as befits women who profess reverential fear for and devotion to God. I Timothy 2:9-10 Amplified)

- Don't compromise your integrity and don't let anyone take it away from you. Your honesty, truthfulness, and righteousness are very important to you and to your station in life. Be honest with yourself and with others. Stand on the truth. (He whose walk is blameless and who does what is righteous, who speaks the truth from his heart. Psalm 15:2 NIV)

- Remember your training. So many times we have a tendency to forget the training we have received when we were younger. Even those of you who live in a dysfunctional home, you can still have a positive future. You can be the one who breaks the cycle. I'm not saying that it is going to be easy, but you can do it. Even surrounded by drugs and alcohol, you can make up your mind that you are going to make something of yourself. There are many times when you will have to encourage yourself, because no one else is going to do it. You don't have to be like dad or mom. Parents, even if they don't say it, want their children to be better than they themselves are. Find yourself a mentor (teacher, counselor, minister) and hold on tight. Those of you, who are living in a home full of love, hold on to it. (I have been reminded of your sincere faith, which first lived in your grandmother Lois and in your mother Eunice and, I am persuaded, now lives in you also. (2 Timothy 1:5 NIV)

- Be proud of who you are. You are somebody, and no one can take that away from you. Sure, you have your own little quirks. You make mistakes. There are times when you fail. This is only being human. Just remember that when you do fall down, don't stay there and waddle in the mud. Pick yourself up and dust yourself off and tell yourself that you need to keep going. Then put some action behind your words. In other words, do something about it. Do something with your life. (I can do everything through Him who gives me strength. Philippians 4:13 NIV)

RACHEL

Romance and tragedy are blessed

(Genesis 29 - 33)

*"And she conceived and bore a son, and said,
God has taken away my reproach."*

Genesis 30:23 (NKJV)

Rachel was the youngest daughter of Laban, and Leah was her older sister. She was a beautiful woman. She met Jacob by a well where she went to water her father's sheep. Jacob was the son of Rebekah, sister to Laban. After Jacob introduced himself with a hug and kiss, Rachel ran to her father to tell him the news of his nephew's arrival. Laban ran out to meet Jacob, embraced and kissed him, and took him to his house.

Laban gave Jacob an opportunity to work for him. Jacob told him that he would not work for wages, but would work for a period of seven years for Rachel's hand in marriage. They both agreed to this arrangement, and Jacob worked very hard during that time.

At the end of the seven years, the marriage ceremony was planned. Rachel was very excited about getting married, but her father had other plans. He tricked Jacob into marrying Leah, the older daughter. Jacob did not realize that he had been tricked until the following morning. He was very angry with Laban, and told him so in no uncertain terms. Laban then told Jacob that, according to their laws, the younger daughter could not marry until the other daughter was married. And, furthermore, Jacob would have to work another seven years for Rachel, even though he was able to marry her after a week.

Leah, but not Rachel, became pregnant four times and had four sons. Since Rachel did not have children, she gave Jacob her handmaiden who became pregnant with two sons. Leah also gave Jacob her handmaiden who had two sons, yet Rachel remained barren. After a while, she finally became pregnant and was so excited that God had found favor with her. She bore a son, which she interpreted as meaning that God had taken away her reproach or disgrace, and she named him Joseph.

After fourteen years of service, Jacob decided to return to Canaan, his home town. Laban did not want him to go because he had become rich with Jacob's help. Jacob made a deal with him and told him how they were going to divide the riches. Laban was upset with the results of the deal and showed his hostility. After twenty years, Jacob decided that it was time to leave. He took his family, his cattle, and his possessions and left secretly while Laban was away. Laban came home and found them gone, went after them and caught them. Jacob was accused of stealing some of Laban's idols from his house. Jacob denied this and even allowed Laban to search the camp. In truth, Rachel was sitting on the idols, but told her father's servants that she was having her period and could not get up. Rachel had stolen the idols. When Jacob later found that she herself had taken the idols, he was very upset and buried them.

Rachel paid for her deceit in childbirth. She went into labor while they were traveling. She had a very hard time and died in childbirth. Before she died, she named her son, "Benoni", which means son of sorrow. Rachel was then buried on the way to Bethlehem.

What kind of questions do you have for Rachel?

QUESTIONS:

Kellie: It must have been love at first sight for Jacob, but how did you feel?

Rachel: I was flattered, but I can't say that I really loved him. I felt that I should be loved since I was so beautiful. My father had spoiled me and I felt that I should be able to get anything that I wanted. In answer to your question, though, it was not love at first sight.

John: What did you really think about Jacob?

Rachel: I thought he was a nice man. He appreciated my beauty. He was in love with me, and he knew how to flatter my ego. I really liked that about him.

Alice: Were you excited when Jacob agreed to work seven years for your hand in marriage?

Rachel: Yes, I was. I thought that he really must love me to go through the trouble of working for seven years just to marry me. I walked around with my head in the clouds for quite some time just thinking about it.

Maria: After the seven years, were you looking forward to your wedding day?

Rachel: Yes! After all, there were no other men around that my father approved. Who else was there to marry?

Kent: How did you feel when your dad did not let you marry Jacob?

Rachel: I was devastated. I cried and cried. I kept pleading with him to let me marry Jacob, but he would not listen. He repeated our customs to me: the younger girl cannot marry until after the older girl is married. I was so upset that I became disrespectful and told him to find her another man. He would not listen to me, and told me to stay away from the ceremony so that I would not be seen.

Alice: How do you think Leah felt with this deception?

Rachel: At the time of the wedding, I didn't know and I really did not care. All I could think about was that she was marrying my Jacob. As I think back on the situation, she had no choice. She had to do what our father told her to do. I also feel that she was in love with Jacob too.

John: Did Jacob say anything to you the next day when he found out that it was Leah and not you?

Rachel: No, but he was very angry. I could tell by the way he and my father were talking. I could not hear what they were saying to each other, but I could read their body language. I'm glad he did not say anything to me because I would probably have just started crying again.

Irene: How did you feel when your father told you that you were getting married a week after Leah's wedding?

Rachel: I could not believe it! I know that the men were allowed to have more than one wife, but I could not believe that I was going to be Jacob's wife. It was a little hurtful that I had to be his second wife, but at least I was going to marry the man that I had come to love.

Irene: Were you jealous of Leah?

Rachel: I guess I was a little jealous of Leah. She was married first, and I wanted to be married. She was married to the man that worked so hard to marry me. She had my man and I wanted him back. But then I began to look at it another way. He had to work seven years for me and was deceived. But he was willing to work seven more years for me, making a total of fourteen years. He worked longer for me than he did for Leah. I must have been special, and I had something to hold over her head.

Alice: How did you and Leah get along after your wedding?

Rachel: We did all right until she started having babies, and I was not able to get pregnant. I was really trying. I was trying to find someone to blame, and I could not blame Jacob because Leah was able to get pregnant. It had to be me. You talk about jealousy; I was very jealous and angry. No one wanted to be around me because I was so miserable. I wanted everyone in the house to be just as miserable as I was. I wanted children so badly that I gave my maidservant to Jacob, and she got pregnant also. Leah saw what I had done and she gave her maidservant to Jacob who also got pregnant. This just made matters worse. I kept picking on Leah while making the others unhappy. It was a rough time.

Kent: Did you feel like God was punishing you?

Rachel: Yes, I did. I was wondering if I was being punished because everyone thought I was so much prettier than Leah. Then I thought that it might be because Jacob loved me more than he did Leah. Finally it came to me that my actions had not been very good ones. My jealousy had gotten out of hand. I was making everyone miserable. I had to ask for forgiveness.

Alice: How did you feel when you became pregnant?

Rachel: I was so very excited. I felt that I had finally been blessed by God. I was going to have a baby and it felt good. Jacob was also happy, even though he had several children already, but none of them were mine. He wanted me to have his child. This was a wonderful pregnancy. God had answered my prayers.

John: Why did you name him Joseph?

Rachel: Well, I wanted to have many more children, and Joseph means "The Lord shall add to me another son." Therefore, I believed that God would bless me with more children, and I was looking forward to it.

Kent: Why did you lie to your father when he was searching for those missing idols?

Rachel: I did not want my children to lose out on their inheritance. Those idols were regarded as indisputable evidence as to the rights and privileges of family ownership, and I wanted to make sure that we had a prosperous journey.

John: What did Jacob do when he found out that you had lied about the idols?

Rachel: He was very angry with me. He did not believe that I could do such a thing, and then turn around and lie about it. He would not listen even when I tried to explain how I felt and what the idols symbolized. It seemed that he had lost some of the trust that he had in me. He was very disappointed.

Irene: What happened to the idols?

Rachel: Jacob took them and buried them in Bethany. I was really glad to get rid of them. You want to know something else? He never told my father what I had done, and he never stopped loving me.

Kellie: Were you pregnant at this time?

Rachel: Yes, I was having my second child, and again I was very excited. Jacob was very happy with my second pregnancy also. But when I went into labor, I had problems. I was having trouble with the delivery. The midwife knew that I was dying, and she told me that I had another son and asked me what I wanted to call him. I called him "Benoni" which means "Son of sorrow." After telling her his name, I died. Jacob re-named him Benjamin.

Maria: What advice would you give to us now?

Rachel: Try to remember the following:

- Beauty is only skin deep. You can be as pretty as a flower on the outside, but it's the beauty that is radiated from the inside that really counts. Outer beauty fades, but inner beauty matures as you age. With makeup, you can enhance your outer beauty, but it requires work to make your inside pretty. It takes humility, love of self and others, compassion, patience, and kindness. (Charm and grace are deceptive, and beauty is vain (because it is not lasting), but a woman who reverently and worshipfully fears the lord, shall be praised. Proverbs 31:30 Amplified)
- Jealousy is hurtful, not only to the other people, but to you also. Jealousy can cause you to become proud, which is also harmful. Pride makes you think you are better than someone else, but you are not. Try walking in someone else's shoes sometime. Who knows, those may be your shoes one day. Remember; try not to think of yourself as being better than anyone else. Don't develop the tendency to look down on someone just because they look or act differently than you do. (For jealousy enrages a man and he will not spare in the day of vengeance. Proverbs 6:24 NAS) (When pride comes, then comes dishonor, But with the humble is wisdom. Proverbs 11:2 NAS)
- Families are important. Love your family. There are so many children who don't know what a real family is. They have been moved from foster home to foster home, abandoned and/or abused, or removed from their homes by the court system. Parents are there to teach and discipline their children with a heart of compassion, kindness, humility, gentleness, and patience. Children are taught to obey and to have respect for their parents, no matter how old they are. In a family, there will be some misunderstandings, but this is to be expected. There should also be love, trust, compassion, heartaches, sorrow, companionship, security, and so much more. So

enjoy and appreciate family while you can. Communicate with each other. Express your feelings. Enjoy each other. (Children, obey your parents in the Lord, for this is right. Honor your father and mother – which is the first commandment with a promise – that it may be well with you and that you many enjoy long life on the earth. Ephesians 6:1-3 NIV) (Fathers, do not provoke your children to anger, but bring them up in the discipline and instruction of the Lord. Ephesians 6:4 NAS)

- Don't straddle the fence. In other words, you can't worship idols and serve God at the same time. I had to make a choice when I was leaving my father, so I did the wrong thing. I took one of my father's prize possessions and, when he asked me about it, I told him that I did not have it. I had an opportunity to make the right choice, but I stole something that did not belong to me. You don't have to be like me. You have been given an opportunity to make choices. Stop and think before making that choice. Weigh your consequences, and then make your choice. (Now fear the Lord and serve him with all faithfulness. Throw away the gods your forefathers worshipped beyond the River and in Egypt, and serve the Lord. But if serving the Lord seems undesirable to you, then choose for yourselves this day whom you will serve . . . But as for me and my household, we will serve the Lord. Joshua 24:14-15 NIV)

- We all have dreams, so don't give up on them. There will be obstacles for you to overcome in order to obtain your dreams, but don't give up. Everything will not go the way that you want all of the time, and you will face disappointments, but keep on working toward your dreams. There are going to be times when you will wonder how you are going to reach those dreams. Everything seems to be going against you. Family is having money problems. You have to change your schedule so that you can help at home or bone up on your studies. Opportunities seem to pass you by, but hang on to your dreams. I was married for many years, wanting children, but it looked like I was never going to have any. I believed that I was cursed, but I held on to my dream. When I had almost given up, I had two sons. So, don't give up. Be honest with yourself. Know your strengths and don't focus on your weaknesses. Your dreams can and will come true. Also, remember the golden rule: "Do unto others as you would have them do unto you." Treat others as you want to be treated. Everyone does not live by this rule, but as long as you are true to yourself, you can and will make it. (For the dream comes through much effort and the voice of a fool through many words. Ecclesiastes 5:3 NAS)

(So then, whatever you desire that others would do to you and for you, even so do also to and for them. For this is (sums up) the Law of the Prophets. Matthew 7:12 Amplified)

HAGAR

Lost a battle, but found a well

(Genesis 16; 21:1-21)

"And the angel of the Lord said to her: Behold, you are with child, And you shall bear a son. You shall call his name Ishmael, Because the Lord has heard your affliction."

Genesis 16:17 (NKJV)

Hagar was an Egyptian slave of Sarah and Abraham while they were in Egypt. They took her with them when they left Egypt, and she became a convert to the worship of the true and living God.

Sarah could not have a baby. She wanted to be able to give a son to Abraham. In that day, they considered a woman to be cursed if she could not have a baby. After living in Canaan for ten years, Sarah made use of a typical ancient Near Eastern custom for a barren wife, which was that the wife authorized her husband to obtain children by sleeping with her personal slave. This is how at the age of 86, Abraham fathered a child with Hagar.

Ancient marriage contracts obligated wives to provide a son for the married couple. If a child was born to a servant or slave, the child would be considered the child of the wife according to the contract. In this way, even a barren woman could fulfill her marital contract.

When Hagar became pregnant, Sarah was jealous. She began to treat her very cruelly. Abraham would not intervene. It went from bad to worse, so Hagar decided to run away because she could no longer handle that type of treatment. An angel of the Lord found her by a spring of water in the wilderness and asked her where she thought she was going. Hagar told him that she was running away from Sarah because of the bad treatment that she had received. The angel told her to go back home and to submit herself to Sarah, and that her descendants would be so great that they would not be able to be counted. He also told Hagar that she was going to have a son whose name was to be Ishmael, because the Lord had heard her sufferings.

This was hard for her to take. She was to return to a place where she had received a lot of abuse. The angel had also told her that her son was going to be wild, and no one was going to accept him. Every mother wants her children to be accepted. Yet she did not hesitate. She did what the angel told her to do and went back home where she gave birth to a son, naming him Ishmael.

Everything seemed to be going well until Sarah became pregnant at the age of ninety-nine years. Ishmael was fourteen at the time and Sarah's first concern was for her new son's status as Abraham's heir, a status that she felt was threatened by Ishmael. The law protected children born to a second wife. It prohibited the disinheriting of a first born son of a slave wife in the event that the barren wife should bear a son later. However, the wife's son would still be the legal firstborn. Hagar and her son could be offered their freedom, in which case they would forfeit Ishmael's inheritance. Hagar did not accept this.

When Sarah weaned Isaac, they had a big celebration. Ishmael began teasing Isaac, and Sarah became very angry. She went and told Abraham to put Hagar and Ishmael out because she did not want Ishmael to be an heir. Abraham was reluctant to do this because Ishmael was his son.

Nevertheless, Abraham got up early the next morning and gave Hagar bread and a container of water and sent them away. They did not have a place to go and quickly used up all of their bread and water. After a while, they were so thirsty that they felt like they could not go any further. Hagar sat Ishmael under a bush. She stepped away because she did not want her son to see her tears. God heard her cry, called her name and asked her what was wrong. Hagar was told to get up and take her son by the hand. The Lord then provided a miracle in the middle of the desert, a well of water! God also told Hagar that Ishmael's descendents would become a great nation.

Hagar and Ishmael lived in the wilderness where he became a great hunter. He later found a wife in Egypt and lived the prophecy.

Can you think of some questions for Hagar?

QUESTIONS:

Kellie: How did Sarah treat you before you became pregnant?

Hagar: She was good to me. She would tell me what to do and I would do it; after all, I was her servant. I was well fed. I had clothes to wear and a decent place to stay. I can truthfully say that I was treated very well.

John: How did Abraham treat you?

Hagar: He did not have much to do with me at first because I was Sarah's servant. I was there mainly to help her with the household chores. After I became pregnant, he was happy and treated me with kindness. He was finally going to be a father.

Alice: How did you feel when you found out that you were pregnant?

Hagar: I was very excited. Being a typical mother-to-be, I wanted to have this baby once I knew I was pregnant. I went through a lot though. I had to sleep with my mistress's husband, something that I really did not want to do, but I had to do as I was told to do. I was not going to give up the chance to have this baby. How was I to know if I would ever have another chance to have my very own child? Yes, I was very excited.

Irene: If you were so excited, why did you run away?

Hagar: Well, a person can only take so much. Sarah was so jealous of my condition, that she became very abusive. She did everything that she could think of to hurt me. You see, there are times when some women become pregnant, that they also become moody, cry a lot, become argumentative, and so much more due to the changes that are taking place in their bodies. With me, it was mostly emotional. I took all I could stand and then it became just too much. I was doing everything that she wanted me to do, but she was never satisfied. It got so bad that I could not take it anymore. I was miserable, so I ran away. I just wanted to keep on running until I could get as far away from Sarah as possible

Kent: How did you feel when the angel stopped you from running?

Hagar: I felt at peace in his presence. It was as if I knew that everything was going to be all right. I was reluctant at first to follow his instructions, but when he assured me that God would work things out, I relented and went back home.

Kent: Were Abraham and Sarah glad to see you?

Hagar: Yes, they were. Sarah put me through some rough times again, but I kept remembering what the angel had told me, and how I felt in his presence. I was now at peace with myself.

Maria: Why did you submit to her wishes anyway?

Hagar: I really did not have much of a choice. Remember, I was a servant and had to do what I was told. I did not want to sleep with Abraham. I respected him for what he was, the husband of my mistress. I wasn't that type of woman. I wanted to have my own husband. I wanted to have my own family, my own place to live, but I had to do as I was told. That was all there was to it

John: Why do you think she treated you so badly? After all, you were doing what she wanted you to do!

Hagar: Well, after I had become pregnant, she felt bad because she was not the one who was pregnant. She did not think that she could have a baby because she was well past child bearing age. She really wanted to have children, but after all this time not being able to conceive, she was desperate. And even though she had given me to Abraham, the idea of my carrying his first child was not pleasant. Abraham was 86 years old, and Sarah probably thought he was too old to produce an off-spring. So, in her mind, there were those two things going against me. And as I began to grow with the baby, it only made matters worse. It certainly wasn't a happy time for her, after all.

Kent: How did you feel when Sarah became pregnant?

Hagar: I was surprised that she became pregnant at her age, but I was happy for her. She had waited a long time to have a baby, and now she was getting her chance. I could not understand how it was possible, but she was happy and I was happy for her. It seemed to ease my circumstances a little also. She began to treat me with kindness.

Kellie: How did Sarah treat you after her son was born?

Hagar: Not too well. She kept watching Ishmael and me. Then sometimes I would see her looking at Abraham when he was with Ishmael. It was as if she felt that he was taking too much time with Ishmael. She went back to her old ways and again became abusive toward me.

Maria: What did you think when Abraham came to you,

giving you bread and a container of water, and told you that you had to leave?

Hagar: What did I think? I thought to myself, I am not going to leave and let my son lose his inheritance. Abraham seemed to be very sorry about the situation, but he was honoring the wishes of his wife. He did not want to have any trouble in his home although I could not believe that he would put out his own son. Putting me out, I could understand, but his first born son? I thought, "no way." I thought he loved Ishmael and would disagree with his wife, but I was so wrong. He had to appease his wife.

Maria: How did you feel?

Hagar: How do you think I felt? I was disgusted, disappointed, broken-hearted, frustrated, and angry. How could a father put his young son, only 14 years old, out of his home? This was a son who had done nothing wrong. And after all that I had been through with his wife's jealousy, things that he knew about, he was still putting me out. After all the hard work that I had done, amid the accusations, my son and I were being sent away with nothing. I could not get over it

John: Did you know where you were going when you left Abraham?

Hagar: I had no idea. I just started walking. I did not know in which direction I was going. I was just getting away from there as fast as I could. When my son was hungry, I fed him some of the bread. When he was thirsty, I gave him some water. After all, Abraham had been kind enough to give us some bread and a container of water. We just kept walking and, after awhile, I realized that we were lost. And by now, we had no food or water. We walked on until we could go no further. My son would ask for water and bread, and I had nothing to give him. What were we supposed to do? There was really nothing that I could do,

so I told him to sit under a shrub. I sat away from him
because I did not want him to see me cry. I was furious
and at my wit's end and I did not want to see my own
son die. I was just about ready to give up when I finally
thought about praying. I began to cry out to God and
He heard me and answered my prayer. I heard the voice
of the angel that I had talked to before. He asked me
why I was so troubled. I told him that my son and I were
out here in the desert with no food or water, and I didn't
want my son to die. The angel told me to take my son
by the hand and stand him up. I did what he told me to
do. Then God performed a miracle. The angel told me to
look around. There in the middle of the desert was a well
of water! I was able to take my container and fill it with
fresh water for us to drink. Again, I was reminded of the
prophecy about my son, how he was going to be blessed
along with his many generations that would follow.

**Irene: I know the day in which we live is so very different
from the day in which you lived, but what advice
could you give us?**

Hagar: It doesn't matter what day you are living in. I had my
problems, you have your problems. I had good times; you
are having some good times. Everything did not go the
way I wanted it to go, and I am sure that everything is
not always going the way that you want it to. My life was
limited. You have so much more to deal with in this day
and time. There is domestic violence, child abuse, mental
illness, peer pressure, HIV/AIDS, suicides, gangs, and
so much more that you have to contend with in your everyday lives. With your electronic devices, you encounter
many things that are not in your best interests.

Some of you don't seem to have any sense of direction
in your young lives. Many of you seem selfish and self-
centered. You think you know it all and are not willing

to listen to good advice. Many of you are turning to drugs instead of to God.

So, what advice can I give you? Let me suggest the following:

- In everything that you do, every place you go, everything you say, remember God. You have an angel with you, and if you listen closely, he will show you the right way to go. Be sure to listen to that angel. Be sure to take out time to think before you act. (Lean on, trust in, and be confident in the Lord with all your heart and mind and do not rely on your own insight or understanding. In all your ways know, recognize, and acknowledge Him, and He will direct and make straight and plain your paths. Proverbs 3:5-6 Amplified)

- You don't have to give up when things get hard for you. When you fail, consider it a learning experience. You don't have to stay down when you fail. Pick yourself up, dust yourself off, and keep on going. Make up your mind not to go that way again. When you get in trouble, trust God to help you. He might not come to your rescue when you think He should, but He will come. (Our fathers trusted in You: They trusted, and You delivered them. They cried to You, and were delivered; They trusted in You, and were not ashamed. Psalms 22:4-5 NKJV)

- Today you are blessed that you can get an education. Don't settle for less. Make something of yourself. (I devoted myself to study and to explore by wisdom all that is done under heaven. What a heavy burden God has laid on me! Ecclesiastes 1:13 NIV)

- Remember, everyday is not going to be sunshine. Some of your days will be stormy. But the same God Who takes care of you during the bright days can and will take care of you during the storm and rain. (The disciples went and woke him, saying, "Master, Master, we're going to drown!" He got up and rebuked the wind and the raging waters; the storm subsided, and all was calm. (Luke 8:24 NIV)

- Finally, remember, God loves you. Look at what happened to me. Things got so bad that all I wanted to do was to run and hide. I ran and ran, but I could not get away because there was something more for me to do. I had to endure a little more suffering and a few more hardships. But God was preparing me for something better. Even though I tried to hide, I learned that you can't hide from God. You can't hide from real love. (But the one who endures to the end, he will be saved. Matthew 24:13 NAS)

DINAH

The woman whose sightseeing had fatal results

(Genesis 34)

"And when Shechem the son of Hamar the Hivite, prince of the country saw her, he took her and lay with her, and violated her.

Genesis 34:2 (nkjv)"

Dinah means justice or one who judges. She was the daughter of Jacob and Leah. She loved to go sightseeing. She was young, daring and curious about things that are outside of her home and in the world around her. One day she slipped away from home to see how the Canaanite girls lived. While Dinah was roaming around, Prince Shechem saw and lusted after her, and then raped her. The young prince fell in love with her and decided to do the right thing by marrying her. The prince's father, King Hamar, spoke with Jacob and his sons about his son's desire to marry Dinah. The marriage was agreed upon, but two of Dinah's brothers, Simeon and Levi decided to attach a condition to the agreement.

All of the men in the city had to be circumcised. King Hamar agreed and all the men were circumcised. When they were recovering from the operation and still in pain, Simeon and Levi killed all the men in the city, including Prince Shechem. They also took every one of the wives and everything that the men of Canaan had. Jacob was very upset with his sons, and Simeon and Levi received a curse instead of a blessing from Jacob just before he died.

QUESTIONS:

Irene: You knew the customs and traditions of your time, so why would you want to wander alone in the city?

Dinah: I was curious. I wasn't really trying to be disobedient. I just wanted to see what the Canaanite girls wore and what they did with some of their time. I also wanted to see some of the sights of the city.

Alice: How did you feel when the prince paid some attention to you?

Dinah: I was flattered. This was the first time that a man, outside of my brothers, took an interest in me. Prince Shechem was really good looking and I just couldn't believe that he would want to talk to me. I had been told that I was pretty by my brothers, but that is what brothers do, or so I thought. When the Prince spoke to me, I was excited.

Maria: When he invited you to the palace, why did you go in?

Dinah: As I said before, I was really flattered. This was the first time that a man noticed me outside of my family. The Prince was so very nice and the palace was right there. After all, how could I pass up this opportunity to see the inside of such a place? I lived on a sheep farm, and when would I have another chance like this? I just had to see the inside, so I decided to go in the palace.

John: I understand that you wanted to see inside a place that you had never seen before, but you knew better

than to accept his invitation. Why would you go into a place with a man you did not know?

Dinah: I guess you can say that I yielded to temptation. It was like I needed to see the inside of the palace. It is true that I knew I should not go anyplace with a man that I did not know, but the palace looked so beautiful. The Prince seemed to be a nice man and he was not trying to put pressure on me, so I thought that I would go in and take a quick tour. Then after the tour, I would go home and I thought no one would know the difference.

Kent: Once, you went into the palace, how did you feel?

Dinah: I was so excited. Everything was beautiful, all of the bright colors, the beautiful furniture, the ornaments, the tapestry. It was all simply breathtaking. I had never seen anything so amazing.

Kellie: How long were you in the palace?

Dinah: Oh, I don't really know exactly how long I was there. All I know is that I saw so many beautiful things that I lost track of the time.

Kellie: During the tour, how did the prince treat you?

Dinah: He was very nice. He answered all of my questions, of which I had many. He would direct me to different the rooms of the palace without touching me. If there was something that he wanted me to see, he would call my attention to it by calling my name and pointing to it. He allowed me to stay as long as I wanted to. He was a complete gentleman at first.

Kent: You had to suspect something when he showed you the bedroom. Usually, when you take a tour of a place, the bedroom that is being used is not a part of the tour. So, didn't you think it was a little improper to be shown his personal bedroom?

Dinah: I was so involved in seeing so much beauty, that I did not think twice about being shown his bedroom. I thought that it was just a part of the tour, especially since the Prince was the one who was personally showing me around.

Maria: Apparently, he must have shown you his bedroom last. Did you have any indication about his intentions at this time?

Dinah: No, I did not. We were talking so much about the palace that I did not notice when he started whispering in my ear. He asked me if I would like to live in the palace. He told me that I could have all of the beautiful things that I had seen. He told me that he thought that I was beautiful, and beauty belonged in a beautiful place. He had one of those soothing voices and the more he talked, the more comfortable I became. I did not realize that I was lying on the bed until he started to undress me. I was frightened and I began to struggle. He then started talking about marriage. This really went to my head. I wanted to be his wife and live in the palace with him. I wanted to become a princess. He raped me.

Irene: How did you feel after he had raped you?

Dinah: I was humiliated. I felt that it was my fault because I let it happen. I felt dirty and betrayed. I wanted to die. All I could think about was what my parents would do when they found out. Also, in my day, a woman could be stoned to death for fornication. I was disgraced and hurting. Then I became angry with the Prince and with myself. I was so ashamed. I did not want to go home, but I didn't have any other place to go. I did not tell anyone what had happened to me.

John: How did your family find out about the rape?

Dinah: Well, the Prince decided that he really wanted to marry me. He asked his father, King Hamar, to talk with my father to get permission to marry me. King Hamar told my father about the rape while asking for my hand in marriage. The King also offered sufficient monetary payment for this marriage. He explained that the Prince had fallen in love with me. My father gave his permission, but my brothers Simeon and Levi had to add a condition before the marriage could take place. I was so upset with them.

Alice: What was the condition?

Dinah: You see, all the Israelite men had to be circumcised. My brothers insisted that all the Canaanite men had to be circumcised because there was no reason for them to be exempt from this process, especially since I was to marry one of them. This had to be done before I could marry the Prince. The King agreed.

Maria: How did you feel when you found out that the Prince wanted to marry you?

Dinah: I was excited. The idea that he loved me, even after he had raped me, and wanted to marry me was exhilarating. I have to admit that I was in love with the Prince too. I would no longer be a disgrace to my family. I would be a princess and living in a beautiful palace. I could hardly believe it. I was really looking forward to the marriage.

Kent: Your brothers, Simeon and Levi, waited until the men had their operation and were too sore to fight back, so that they could kill them. How did this make you feel?

Dinah: I was devastated. I was ready to marry, looking forward to it, and they had decided to kill my Prince and all the Canaanite men. It was so wrong. I didn't understand how they could do such a thing. Sure, I was raped, but the stigma was being erased because I was going to marry the man who raped me. I was going to be a wife and not a disgrace to my family. My opportunity to live a decent life was ruined. Who would want to marry a woman who had been raped in my day? No one!

Kellie: Do you have any advice to give to us?

Dinah: Yes, I do.

- There are times when you may be envious of what others have. But, if you have a place to live, food to eat, clothes to wear, and love of a parent or parents, you are truly blessed. Don't try to live above your means. Don't try to be more than you are just because someone has more than you. Remember, there are some who wish they could have what you have, and there are some who are worse off than you. (Keep your lives free from the love of money and be content with what you have, because God has said, "Never will I leave you, never will I forsake you. Hebrews 13:5 NIV")

- Girls, be careful of boys with flattering words. Be sure that the boys you date know and understand your values. Be sure that their values match yours. Know who you are and stay away from boys who want you to be something that you are not. Be aware of your surroundings. Have your cell phone set for emergency numbers so all you have to do is hit one number for help. Have a number for 911 and another for your parents. If you are ever assaulted, tell someone. Don't be embarrassed and don't bathe or destroy your clothing before turning them over to the police. Don't blame yourself because it is not your fault in most cases. (Do not be yoked together with unbelievers. For what do righteousness and wickedness have in common? Or what fellowship can light have with darkness? What harmony is there between Christ and Belial? What does a believer have in common with an unbeliever? II Corinthians 6:14-15 NIV)

- Be ready to accept the consequences of your actions. So many times we act and react to situations, and when things don't go the way we want them to, you blame others. If you are told no by a parent and you feel that they don't know what they are talking about, you often disagree. When things go wrong or you are caught doing wrong, you complain that your punishment is too hard. You are the one who decided to do what you knew was wrong, so you should not complain about the consequences of your behavior. (Make no mistake: God is not mocked, for a person will reap only what he sows because the one who sows for his flesh will reap corruption from the flesh, but the one who sows for the spirit will reap eternal life from the spirit. Galatians 6:7-8 NAB)

- Don't allow sexual passion to boil over into evil actions. Passion must be controlled. Sometimes it only starts with a casual kiss. This feels good to you and you want it to continue. You find yourself becoming so involved that you don't want to stop. You know deep down that you need to stop, but you, your partner, or both of you can't or are not willing to call a halt. After the sexual act, you may feel guilty or even unclean if it's the first time. (Flee from sexual immorality. All other sins a man commits are outside his body, but he who sins sexually sins against his own body. Do you not know that your body is a temple of the Holy Spirit, who is in you, whom you have received from God? You are not your own: you were brought at a price. Therefore, honor God in your body.

I Corinthians 6:18-20 NIV)

- Be faithful to your family's obligations. Your parents have developed rules for you to follow. You might not agree with them at all times. You might not like all of the rules. You might think that your parents are too strict and unreasonable. But you have a moral obligation, as well as a responsibility to follow their rules, and to accept any consequence for not obeying them. This can be hard for you sometimes. Try to pick a time when you and your parents can talk together constructively. Be sure that you are willing to listen to their point of view. (Children, be obedient to your parents in all things, for this is well pleasing to the Lord. Colossians 3:20 NAS)

TAMAR

The woman with a pathetic History

Genesis 38:15-24

When she was brought out, she sent to her father-in-law, saying, "By the man to whom these belong, I am with child. And she said, "Please determine whose these are – the signet and cord, and staff."

Genesis 38:25 (NIV)

The women in Canaan were supposed to marry and have children in order to carry on the family line. The bride was expected to be a virgin on her bridal night. If it was found that she had had sex before the marriage, she was to be executed.

Judah had three sons. Tamar was the wife of the oldest son, Er. He died before they had any children. Judah then told his next oldest son, Onan, to marry her. Onan did so, but he refused to father a child with her because it would not be his, but Er's. In those days, when a son dies without fathering a child, who ever marries the widow of that man must name the child after the widow's first husband so that his family line is maintained. Onan wanted the child for himself and not for his brother. He too died before Tamar could be impregnated. Judah promised Tamar that if she would stay a widow, when his youngest son, Shelah, was grown, he would marry her. She was to return to her father's house and remain a widow.

Shelah grew up, but he did not marry Tamar. When Tamar found out that Shelah had married someone else and that Judah had broken his promise, she was very upset. She knew Judah's routine, so she decided to sit by the road as a harlot, and wait for Judah to pass by. She covered her face so that he could not recognize her. Judah was lonely, so he asked her to go with him. Before she would go, she asked him how much he was willing to pay. He offered her a sheep, but she said that that was not enough. She asked him to give her his signet and his staff. His signet was very important because it was a seal with his name or emblem worn around his neck. This was indispensable for men of wealth or position as it was used on all legal documents for certification. Judah foolishly gave it to her. When he went looking for her the next day to get his possessions back, he could not find her, so his possessions were lost to him.

Three months later, Judah was told that his former daughter-in-law was pregnant. Judah was ready to have her executed. When she was brought forward, she showed Judah the signet, the cord, and the staff, indicating that he was the father of her child. Judah had to acknowledge that those were his possessions and that he had treated Tamar wrong. He told the men that she was a better person than he was because he did not keep his promises.

Judah took her to his house, but he never slept with her again. At the end of her pregnancy, Tamar had twins and named them Pharez and Zarah. Pharex means the cause of her sin and Zarah means a rising light of dawn.

QUESTIONS:

Irene: Why did you believe Judah when he told you that he was going to give Shelah, his third son, to you?

Tamar: Well, since he had given me his second son, I just assumed he was a man of his word. He had never let me down, so I trusted him. I really had no reason to suspect anything different.

Kellie: How did you feel when you found out that you would not be given to his third son?

Tamar: I was very angry after waiting several years for him to grow up, and then to find out that I was not going to become his wife. Not only was I angry, but I was determined to get even with Judah.

John: Why did you choose prostitution?

Tamar: You see, in my day I did not have much choice. I had lost two husbands. I had a father-in-law who did not keep his promises. I was living at home. I could not work and make my own living. Women were supposed to marry and have babies, and I had neither. I was lost and I felt that there was nothing more for me to do.

Alice: I noticed that you knew how prostitutes dressed. Why was this?

Tamar: Although I lived a sheltered life, I had seen these women on the streets, so I knew I had to dress. All I had to do was to go through my wardrobe and find some of my clothes that were similar to the ones a prostitute wore. It was simple enough.

Kent: How did you know where Judah would be at that time of day?

Tamar: After all, I was married to two of his sons. I knew where he kept his sheep. I knew the times of day that he went to take care of his sheep, so all I had to do was to go to the place and wait beside the road.

Maria: How did you feel seducing your ex-father-in-law?

Tamar: It really didn't bother me much. I kept thinking about what he had done to me, and I felt that he was getting exactly what he deserved.

Kent: Why did you ask for his signet, cord, and bracelet for your services?

Tamar: I wanted to make sure that he would pay greatly for my services, and by asking him for his signet, cord, and bracelet, it would show me how much he really wanted me. It also assured me that if I did become pregnant, I would be able to prove who the baby's father was. In this way, I would not be put to death for prostitution. I was determined not only to save my life, but to expose my former father-in-law because of what he had done to me.

John: How did you feel when you found out you were pregnant?

Tamar: I was excited at first. I was finally going to have a baby. Then I became afraid. What was going to happen to me when the people found out? Everyone knew I wasn't married. Then I remember the signet, bracelet, and cord. I could use them for my life.

Irene: After the sexual encounter with your father-in-law, where did you go?

Tamar: I went back home. I no other place to go. When I got there, I acted like nothing had happened. I knew that Judah would look for me because I had taken his most prized possession. He had to get them back. Since he did not know who I was, I figured that he would not even question me.

Alice: I still can't understand why he did not know it was you.

Tamar: Well, I was so determined to keep my identity a secret that I refused to remove my veil. He never had the chance to see my face.

Kellie: How did you feel when you confronted Judah with the evidence that he was the father of your babies?

Tamar: I was ecstatic. I had my revenge. You should have seen his face. It was something to see. He was so ashamed of what he had done. When they wanted to kill me, he had to speak up. He was man enough to say that it was his fault and not mine.

John: So Judah was an honorable man after all.

Tamar: Well, he was honorable enough to stand up and admit when he was wrong. Honorable in the beginning, no, but when it really counted, yes.

Maria: What advice would you give us now?

Tamar:

- Girls, don't believe all the promises most men make, especially if you do not know the men personally. There are times when you even have to be careful of promises made by men you think you know. Sometimes these promises are given for the wrong reasons. Some men will say anything to get what they want. (It is better to trust in the Lord than to put confidence in man. Psalm 118:8 NKJV)
- You don't have to become promiscuous to get and/ or keep a man. When they get tired of you, they will find another one to take your place. Sometimes, while they are with you, they have another girl on the side. (Flee from sexual immorality. All other sins a man commits are outside his body, but he who sins sexually sins against his own body. Do you not know that your body is a temple of the Holy Spirit, who is in you, whom you have received from God? You are not your own, you were bought at a price. Therefore honor God with your body. I Corinthians 6:18-20 NIV)
- Love your family. Sometimes you won't like what is going on within your own family. You won't agree with everything that is being said. There may be times

when you may feel unloved, but this is normal in many families. Don't try to justify your bad actions just because you have been hurt by someone within your family. Remember, that if your family is doing the best that it can and showing their love, you are truly blessed. (Finally, all of you, live in harmony with one another, be sympathetic, love as brothers, be compassionate and humble. Do not repay evil with evil, or insult with insult, but with blessing, because to this you were called so that you may inherit a blessing. I Peter 3:8-9 NIV)

- Revenge can backfire. I was out for revenge against Judah, but I didn't really count on getting pregnant. It only took one time and I was pregnant. I didn't know what would become of me. I was not a prostitute. Some prostitutes were temple prostitutes, supported by offerings, while others were common prostitutes supported by the men who used their services. Their children were nobody's heirs, and the men who hired these prostitutes adulterated nobody's bloodlines. Even though I had Judah's family articles, I could not be sure that he would admit to the intercourse and accept me and my babies into his family. (Never take your own revenge, beloved, but leave room for the wrath of God, for it is written, "Vengeance is mine, I will repay," says the Lord. Romans 12:19 NAS)

- Bitterness vs. forgiveness. It is easy to become bitter when you have been hurt, especially by someone you love. You can't believe that that person would treat you the way he or she did and then turn his or her back on you. After all that you had in common with this person, you counted him or her as a friend and you were betrayed. You have a right to be bitter. But don't hold on to your bitterness. Ask God's help in showing you how to forgive. (If you forgive others their transgressions, your heavenly Father will forgive you. But if you do not forgive others, neither will your Father forgive your transgressions. Matthew 6:14-15 NAB)

BATHSHEBA

Her beauty resulted in adultery and murder

(2 Samuel 11–12)

"Then it happened one evening that David arose from his bed and walked on the roof of the king's house. And from the roof he saw a woman bathing and the woman was very beautiful to behold."

2 Samuel 11:2 (NKJV)

Bathsheba was raised in a God-fearing family. Her father's name was Eliam. She married a soldier named Uriah who was gone most of the time, fighting in wars for King David.

One day Bathsheba decided to take a bath on the roof, where King David saw her and decided that he wanted her for himself. He seduced her and Bathsheba became pregnant. When the king learned she was pregnant, he sent for her husband, Uriah, and told him to go home to his wife. But Uriah did not sleep with his wife; instead, he slept out doors. When asked why he did not stay with his wife, he said that he did not think it was right for him to enjoy the comforts of home while the other soldiers were on the battlefield. King David then told the commander to be sure to place Uriah on the front lines so that he could be killed. Uriah died fighting in the king's war.

After a short period of mourning, David married Bathsheba. The baby was very sick. David fasted and prayed, but within a week, the baby died. Soon after, Bathsheba had another son and called him Solomon. Bathsheba also had four more sons with King David.

King David gave Bathsheba a promise that Solomon would be the next king. It was a tradition that the first born son of a king would be the next king. Solomon was not the first born. When David was so old that he could not do his kingly duties, his oldest son took over the king's duties. But Bathsheba reminded David of his promise, so that when David died Solomon became king. Bathsheba lived to see a portion of Solomon's rule.

What questions would you have for Bathsheba?

QUESTIONS:

John: You said that you were brought up in a god-fearing home. If this is true, why should you take your clothes off in public, even if it was on a roof?

Bathsheba: Well, it was hot and I wanted to cool off. I looked around to make sure no one was watching. I would not have taken my clothes off if I had known that the king was watching. I'm sure that the king had probably gone to his roof after I started bathing.

Maria: I realize that you had to obey the king's summons, but why did you sleep with him?

Bathsheba: I really don't know. I guess I was so infatuated with the king that we just kept talking and talking and, before I knew it, I was in bed with him. He was very good at seducing. He kept using flattery, and I was so pleased he desired me, that I just got carried away.

Kent: Did you even think about your husband while you were with the king?

Bathsheba: I did think about him at first, but like I said, the king was very good with his   seduction and I forgot about my husband. The king knew what he wanted, and he was determined to get it. I was so wrapped up in what he was doing to me that I just completely forgot all about my husband.

Kellie: How did you feel afterwards when you left the king's palace?

Bathsheba: I had a guilty conscience. I kept questioning myself. How could I have been gullible? What was I thinking? What could I say to my husband? Nothing, really! I could not say that I had an affair with the king, at least not to my husband. I decided to do nothing.

Irene: What did you do when you discovered you were pregnant?

Bathsheba: I sent word to King David at once because I wanted him to know that I was pregnant. I knew that it had to be his baby because I had not slept with my husband for several months. There was no one to turn to. My husband was away fighting in the war. I had no family close by. The king was the only one I could reach out to, and, after all, it was entirely his fault. He was the one who seduced me. He was the one who summoned me, and I really was in trouble.

Kent: What do you mean, it was entirely his fault? It takes two to tangle!

Bathsheba: You are right. Even though I had to obey his summons, I did not have to give in. I know that I could have resisted. I was very vulnerable and lonely but, at the time, all I could think about was the fact that I was pregnant, and my husband had been away for some time. You talk about feeling guilty, I was desperate. I felt so bad that I had committed adultery.

Alice: How did you feel when your husband returned?

Bathsheba: I was scared and worried at the same time. What if he had found out that I was pregnant? What would I do? I made up my mind to seduce my husband. I fixed him his favorite meal, dressed in my most provocative clothes, and talked and laughed with him. We were having a good time so I decided to go to bed. I waited up for him but he never came. When I went looking for him, I could not find him. I must have fallen asleep because when I woke up, it was morning. My husband Uriah had never slept with me. Now I was really scared.

Irene: What did you do?

Bathsheba: What could I do? My husband refused to sleep with me. When I asked him why, he stated that he did not think it was right for him to enjoy the comforts of home when his fellow soldiers were enduring hardships on the battlefield. I then remembered how patriotic Uriah was and realized that he would never sleep with me as long as his men were at war. I was pregnant, with nowhere to turn, and a husband who refused to comfort and sleep with me.

Maria: What happened then?

Bathsheba: Uriah came to me and told me that he had orders to return to the battlefield. He told me good-bye and left. The next thing I knew, he was gone. Later that week, I heard that he had been killed while fighting the enemy.

Kent: You did not accomplish anything. All your plans didn't work out. Now your husband was dead and you were carrying an illegitimate baby. What did you do?

Bathsheba: I was devastated. I just sat there and cried. While I pitied myself, one of the king's men came to get me. Again, I was summoned to the king's palace. This time I was told that I was to get married. I was trying to figure out to whom I was supposed to marry, when the king came in and told me that he and I were getting married. We were married very quietly. I was then content. I was now a queen, a very pregnant queen for sure, but a queen nevertheless.

Kellie: You had a son, but he died soon after childbirth. What were you thinking?

Bathsheba: I was hurting. I had just lost my firstborn son. No mother wants to lose her baby. It really hurts. It's a terrible thing to have to go through. But my pain went a little further. I kept remembering that I had committed adultery. My baby was conceived through an adulterous act. I felt like my baby deserved to die, and I wanted to die. You talk about a pity party, I was really having one. I did not want to see anyone. I did not want to talk to anyone. I felt like I was an evil person. I absolutely deserved what was happening to me.

Alice: When you found out that you were pregnant again, how did you feel?

Bathsheba: I was scared and very happy at the very same time. I did not want this baby to die. I prayed a lot. I wanted a healthy baby. That is just what I got, a very healthy baby. When my second son was born, I named him Solomon. After his birth, I had four more sons.

John: How did you convince King David to give his throne to Solomon? After all, according to tradition, the throne usually goes to the oldest son, and Solomon was not the oldest son.

Bathsheba: I still had some influence over David. You see, I was a model wife and I tried to please him in every way. Therefore, I convinced David to give me a promise that my son would be the next king. David was now sick and could not perform his kingly duties, so his oldest son,

Adonijah, took over those duties. I went to David and reminded him of his promise. He kept his word and my Solomon became the next king.

Alice: And what is your advice to us?

Bathsheba: Think about the following:

- Don't let one mistake ruin your whole life. Remember, I committed adultery and, because of that, my husband was killed and my first born son died after childbirth. I was devastated and would have continued on a downhill trend if I had not had someone with whom to share my mistake. I had to live with it, but I did not let it be the ruler of my life. Use each mistake as a guide to future and better conduct. I did not make the same mistake twice. I was faithful to David until death. If you make mistakes, learn from them. Pick yourself up and remind yourself what you did and why you did it, then determine that you will not go that route again. Above all, don't blame others for your mistakes. There should be no one who can really make you do anything wrong. Ultimately, you are the only one who can make that final choice. (For each one should carry his own load. Galatians 6:5 NIV)
- Good people can do very bad things. I was a good wife who got caught up in a bad situation. I pitied myself. No, it was not intentional, but I was in the wrong place at the wrong time. Don't judge everyone based on your own imperfections. No one is perfect and sometimes they will slip. Just because you slipped once does not mean that you are bad. There is always some good in everyone. (He who covers his transgressions will not prosper, but whoever confesses and forsakes his sins will obtain mercy. Proverbs 28:13 Amplified)
- Forgive others. If someone has done you a wrong and has asked for your forgiveness, forgive them. It might be hard, but forgive them. You might feel that some

time away from them would help, but forgive them. If they don't ask for forgiveness, don't hold a grudge against them, forgive them anyway. Once you have done this, you will be better able to forgive yourself. Forgive yourself. There are too many people who are living with the guilt of mistakes that they made while they were young. They have never forgiven themselves. It's time to forgive and to let go. This is not always easy either, but it is possible. You will turn out all right. Now live the rest of your life in the best possible way. And respect yourself. (Do not take revenge, my friends, but leave room for God's wrath, for it is written: "It is mine to avenge: I will repay," says the Lord. On the contrary: "If your enemy is hungry, feed him; drink; in doing this you will heap burning coals on his head." Romans 12:19-20 NIV)

- Don't forget your early training. If you were brought up or are being brought up in a God-fearing home, don't forget the prayers you prayed, the church services you attended, the Bible scriptures you read, and the love you were shown. Wherever you are, whatever you are doing, be sure to keep God in the picture and He will be there for you. If you were brought up in a dysfunctional home where there was abuse, yelling, alcoholism, drugs, and more, make up your mind that you will not get involved. You can see where it is taking those in your family. They are not happy. You can break the cycle. Find someone you can talk to, a counselor, a friend, a pastor, a priest, a rabbi, or a responsible adult. Let them know that you need and want help, and they will stand with you. They will help you break the cycle. (Love the Lord your God with all your heart and with all your soul and with all your strength. These commandments that I give you today are to be upon your hearts. Impress them on your children. Talk about them when you sit at home and when you walk along the road, when you lie down and when you get up. Deuteronomy 6:5-7 NIV) (But if anyone does not provide for his own and especially for those of his household, he has denied the faith and is worse than an unbeliever. I Timothy 5:8 NAS)

- Accept your responsibilities. You are responsible to yourself first. You know right from wrong. You have choices to make. You have to live with the choices that you make. Sometimes you won't like the choices that you make, but always remember that you are the one who has to live with them. (So every one of us shall give account of himself to God. Romans 14:12 KJV)

  •

RUTH

Rose from obscurity to riches

(Ruth 1-4)

"But Ruth said: Entreat me not to leave you, Or to turn back from following after you; For wherever you go, I will go; And wherever you lodge, I will lodge; Your people shall be my people, and your God, my God."

Ruth 1:16 (NKJV)

Ruth was a woman who rose from obscurity to riches. She was beautiful and from the town of Moab, which is only about thirty miles from Bethlehem. Her story takes place during the time of the judges.

We meet Ruth when she was a young widow, one of the daughter-in-laws of Naomi. She had been married for ten years and there were no children. She did not drown herself in self-pity nor did she manifest the bitterness that had gripped Naomi. She maintained a sense of poise and serenity. Ruth also calmly accepted the divine will of God.

Ruth was a faithful daughter-in-law, bound to her mother-in-law by a common grief. Naomi had lost both of her sons and her husband. When Naomi decided to return to her homeland, Bethlehem, Ruth was willing to leave her own land, her friends and her relatives, to share an unknown future with Naomi. This was pure and unselfish devotion on her part, as well as quiet commitment.

Ruth was brought up in a heathen country where idolatry was practiced. She was a member of a degenerate Moabite tribe. When she decided to go to Bethlehem with her mother-in-law, she had to leave her religious beliefs behind. Everything that she knew of her culture had to be left behind. She was going into a new land where things would be different.

She became a determined convert, and embraced the same religion as Naomi, serving the true and living God. Casting off her idolatry, Ruth turned to the beauty and blessedness of this religion. Her faith took on the form of a quiet humble service, and this remained untainted by any trace of pride or of spiritual self-importance. Ruth had a beautiful heart, a generosity of soul, a firm sense of duty, and a meekness that was pure.

When they arrived in Bethlehem, they found only poverty. Naomi left with much, but she returned to nothing. She had only a house that needed some repair because it had been neglected for so many years. There was nothing for them to eat. What were they to do? Harvest times were the most important times in the life of the Jews. In those days, the poor and the outcast were allowed to walk behind the men that cut the barley and pick up the golden sheaves that were left. According to the Jewish law, it was a custom for the corner of the fields to be left for the poor, and a sheaf was also to remain there for them.

Naomi told Ruth that, in order for them to survive, she must go out into the fields and glean. Ruth did not hesitate, but followed Naomi's instructions even though she had not done that kind of work before. She had never been that poor. She did not even think about the fact that she was a stranger in a strange land, or whether or not she would be accepted by the others who were also gleaning. She got up the next morning, went to the fields, and took home some of the golden sheaves so that she and her mother-in-law could eat.

She did not stop to find out who owned the field. The owner happened to be a godly man by the name of Boaz, who would go out into his fields to make sure that everything was going as it should.

He noticed Ruth because she was a foreigner and a beautiful woman, and asked about her. He was told who she was and to whom she was related. Naomi, through marriage, just happened to be related to him. According to the kinsman-redeemer law, Boaz could buy Naomi's property and marry Ruth. There was a closer relative to Naomi, but he did not wish to buy the land. Boaz then was able to buy the land and marry Ruth.

This marriage was blessed with a son, and they named him Obed, which means "servant who worships." Because of her unselfish loyalty toward Naomi, she made sure that Obed also was a part of Naomi's life. Naomi finally had a grandchild to love and to help raise. Ruth, who was Gentile by birth, became the chosen line through which, later, the Savior of the world appeared.

The book of Ruth is a story of love, loyalty and redemption. Ruth left all that she knew to go with Naomi to a strange land. This was a relationship where there was a strong mutual commitment, where they worked together to do what was best for the other person, and where the strongest bond of all was their faith in God. Through Ruth's self-giving love, God brought great blessings out of Naomi's tragedy.

It's time to think about a question that you could ask Ruth.

QUESTIONS:

Maria: How did you feel about leaving your hometown and the customs that you were used to?

Ruth: At that time, I was not thinking about myself. I was looking at a woman who had lost more than I had and wanted to go home. I felt that I could not let her go by herself. What was she to do? I did not know what was waiting for her, but I just could not let her go alone. Within myself I felt that she needed me, and I knew that I could be a help to her. So I had made up my mind and told Naomi the following:

- I wanted her to know that where she went, I was willing to go.
- I wanted her to know that where she lived, I was willing to live there also.
- I wanted her to know that her people would be my people.
- I wanted her to know that her God would be my God.
- I wanted her to know that where she died, I would die and be buried.
- I made a promise to God that if I did not keep all of these promises, and much more, then let only death separate us and nothing else.

Irene: You were married for ten years without having any children. After all, there was a stigma attached to not having children. How did you feel about being childless, and did you want any children?

Ruth: Yes, I wanted children. I very much wanted to have a child. I did not like to be looked upon as being cursed because I was barren. I wanted so much to be able to give my husband a son so that his name could be carried on for another generation. I wanted Naomi to have a grandchild that she could cherish, especially after the loss of her husband. Being in the situation where I did not conceive was devastating to me. It was an extra hardship when my first husband died, and I had no children with which to remember him. This was very hurtful and depressing. I never thought that I would marry again. Among my own people, who would want to marry me? After all, I was cursed because I bore my husband of ten years   no children. It was not his fault. I was the woman, so it was my fault. It was my shame to bear and I had to bear it alone.

Kent: What did you think of Bethlehem when you first saw it?

Ruth: I had heard so much about Bethlehem from Naomi that

I was looking forward to seeing it. I was a little disappointed when I saw the house in which we were to live.
Yet the people were very welcoming, and I felt that we
could make it there. The land itself was not so different
from my own town; after all, we were only separated by
thirty miles. It was the time of harvest, and I was used to
seeing the people working in the fields and going about
their daily lives.

**John: How did you feel when you got to Bethlehem and saw
the evidence of her situation? Were you discouraged?
I am quite sure that she had told you some good
things about her homeland.**

Ruth: I was not discouraged. I was a little frightened because I
was able to see for myself what I had gotten into. I was
also glad that I had come because it made me realize that
Naomi could not make it by herself. I felt a little uneasy
though, because I was in a strange land and did not
know the customs. I also sensed in Naomi her frustration when she saw what she had returned to. The house
had been neglected. There was no food. She had left
Bethlehem with much and returned to nothing. When I
saw this, I was really glad that I came so that I could be a
help to her.

**Kellie: What was your reaction when Naomi told you that
you would have to go and work in the fields?**

Ruth: I was disappointed, but I understood the situation. Someone had to work and we had to eat. I was afraid because
I had never worked in the field before. I was used to
doing housework, going to the well for water, cooking
meals, and taking care of my husband. When it came to
work outside of the home, my husband had done that. So
the idea of my going out into the field to work was very
frightening. Naomi gave me some good instructions on
what I had to do in the fields, and it did not seem to be

so hard. All I was doing was walking behind the reapers and collecting sheaves. At first I was a little confused as to which ones I was supposed to pick up, but I learned by watching others.

Alice: What did you think of Boaz when you first saw him?

Ruth: I really did not notice him very much except for the kindness he was showing to workers that were in the field. I did not know who he was, but he looked as if he were important. While he was walking in the fields, he took the time to speak to even the poorest looking person. This let me know that he was a good man. As far as his looks, well, there was not anything very special about them. After all, my husband had been a handsome man and, to me, there was no one who could compare to him. After seeing Boaz on several occasions, I noticed there was an inner beauty in him that you don't see in many men. He was not afraid to show his gentle side. He seemed to look at each person as an equal. He even spoke to me, a foreigner, and this made me feel appreciated. I was able to go home and tell Naomi all about him.

Kellie: What did Boaz say to you when you were in the field?

Ruth: He gave me a six-fold message:

- He told me to listen to what he had to say.
- I was not to go into any other field to glean.
- I was to stay close to his maids and not to leave the field for any reason.
- Follow the maidens and the reapers and go behind them to glean.
- Don't be afraid of his young men, for he had told them not to touch me.
- When I got thirsty, I was to go to the vessels and drink from the ones which the young men had drawn.

Alice: How did you feel when you found out that he was a distant relative of Naomi's husband? I am sure that she told you about the traditions of her people when a wife does not have a child to carry on the family name.

Ruth: I did not have any high hopes because, after all, I was a foreigner. Although he was a kind man that did not mean that he was willing to abide by that tradition that was a part of his culture. There were many women of his own kind that he could have married, and he had the best excuse in the world not to marry me. In my case, he was not actually bound by any tradition. But after I had met him, I began to think of the advantages of being married to him. He was such a wonderful man, that I knew that it would be a privilege for him even to consider marrying me. In fact, I began to hope that he might think about it.

Kent: That's very interesting. Do you know the steps that Boaz had to take as a part of the "kinsman redemption" law?

Ruth: The part of the "kinsman redemption" law that applies to Boaz is that he had to be sure Naomi's closest male relative gave up his right to marry Ruth and buy back her property. Then once Boaz married her, he had an undeniable right to buy back the deceased kinsman's, the son of Naomi, property.

These were the seven steps to my kinsman redemption:
- Getting witnesses to confirm every transition between all parties involved as possible redeemers.
- Getting an agreement to determine which closest kinsman should be the redeemer.
- This kinsman, not wanting to marry me, had to give up the right to marry the widow and redeem her dead husband's property. This was done in a special ceremony

in which he would take off one of his shoes to show that he released his right to marry the widow and receive the property. This would give another man, in my case, Boaz, the right of redemption.

- The redemption of the inheritance itself is settled.
- Marriage is arranged between the redeemer, and the wife of the dead one, to raise any future children that will continue the name of the dead husband.
- There are at least three witnesses who must confess that they are in agreement with the arrangements.
- The blessing is given to the marriage.

John: What blessing was given to Boaz and Ruth on their marriage?

Ruth: It was beautiful. The Lord was called upon in the marriage to make a fruitful house like that of Jacob and his wives; to make the new family worthy of being inhabitants in Israel; and to make them famous in Bethlehem and like the house of Parez.

Kellie: Were you happy in your marriage with Boaz?

Ruth: Yes, I was very happy. You see, our marriage was founded on an appreciation for each other as individuals. Our love grew out of this commitment to values for more than good looks. Boaz treated me favorably. He had a good reputation among his fellow men. He had a marvelous capacity for love and loyalty toward me. He was also willing to work hard to support both me and Naomi. Who could not be happy with a man like that?

Maria: After you married Boaz and found out that you were pregnant, were you excited? Also, did this make you feel better about yourself because it was not your fault that you had not had a baby before?

Ruth: I was ecstatic. I was pregnant. I was going to have a baby. I was not barren. I was giving Boaz what he wanted. I was not cursed, I was a whole woman, and I was doing what I was put on this earth for, to have children. No one could have been happier than I was.

John: Why did you include Naomi in your relationship with Boaz? You were now a part of your husband's family. You did not have to let Naomi help you take care of your son. In fact, you literally acted as if she were the real grandmother.

Ruth: Naomi was always, and always would be, my mother-in-law. If it had not been for her, I would not be as happy as I am. I would not have met Boaz. I would not have married him, and I would not have had a son. I owe it all to her and to her God, which is the only true and living God. This is the God that I now serve. He put this wonderful woman in my life. She was very special to me, and she always treated me as if I were her daughter, not her daughter-in-law. She showed me love and taught me many things about her culture, and she accepted me for being me. I did not have to change. I changed because of her and because I wanted to change. Another reason was that according to the "kinsman redemption," my son was to be her grandson. This was the child that was to be raised on behalf of my dead husband. Yes, I had to keep this special woman in my life. I wanted my son to experience the love and compassion of Naomi. My husband did not object because he saw in Naomi many of the things that I saw in her. We had a wonderful life together, all of us!

Kellie: Looking back over your life, what can you say that might help us in our lives today?

Ruth: Let me just say this:

- You need to be the kind of person that draws others to God, so do your best to keep a good reputation. Watch yourself. Be sure that your actions speak louder than your words. There are too many people who say that they care, using words, but their actions show otherwise. Remember a good reputation can open doors for you. (A good name is rather to be chosen than great riches, and loving favor rather than silver and gold. Proverbs 22:1 KJV)

• There are going to be sorrows in your life, but these can be turned into joy as long as you put your trust in God. Just keep on doing the best that you can, and even in the worst situations there can be a little ray of sunshine. I lost a husband, but look at all that I gained. I gained a loving mother-in-law, another husband, a son and the faith in a true and living God. God will keep you in perfect peace if you keep your mind centered on Him. But if you truly open his voice and all that I say, then I will be an enemy to your enemies and an adversary to your adversaries. Exodus 23:22 NAS)

• You can overcome any situation. You are going to fall down, but you don't have to stay down. You are going to make mistakes, but learn from your mistakes. Believers will have adversities as well as non-believers, but remember that God will never forsake or leave you. Just hold on, and things will work out all right. It might not be like you want it, but it will be for the best. (Test everything. Hold on to the good. Avoid every kind of evil. I Thessalonians 5:21-22 NIV)

• Learn to appreciate those who are older and/or more experienced than you are. Listen to what they have to say. Why should you have to experience everything that is negative? Let them tell you of their experiences and learn from them. Why do you have to experience drugs, alcohol, promiscuity, etc. when you can learn from other's lives? (Young men, in the same way be submissive to those who are older. All of you, clothe yourself with humility toward one another, because "God opposes the proud but gives grace to the humble." Humble yourselves, therefore, under God's mighty hand, that he may lift you up in due time. I Peter 5:5 6 NIV)

- There are many times when God uses our adversities for His opportunities. These can be times when His great redemptive power continues to cause all things to work out for our good in times of trouble. Just remember to put your trust in God, and even when things get so hard that you don't know how you are going to make it, God will step in every time and give you peace, deep inside. The situation has not changed. The people have not changed. But you have changed, because you are not upset about things any more. You can say to yourself that God is working on the situation, so things will be alright. (Commit your way to the Lord; trust in him and he will do this; He will make your righteousness shine like the dawn, the justice of your cause like the noonday sun. Be still before the Lord and wait patiently for him; do not fret when men succeed in their ways, when they carry out their wicked schemes. For evil men will be cut off, but those who hope in the Lord will inherit the land. Psalms 37:5- 7, 9 NIV)

-

DELILAH

Betrayed her husband for silver

(Judges 16:4-21)

*"And it came to pass, when she pestered him dai-
ly with her words and pressed him, so that his soul was
vexed to death, that he told her all his heart,"*

Judges 16:16-17a (NKJV)

Samson was consecrated to God as a Nazarene from birth,
meaning he could not cut his hair nor drink wine. He was a judge,
known for his extraordinary physical strength. He was to begin
the deliverance of the people of Israel from the Philistines and,
on his own, had killed 1000 Philistines with a donkey's jawbone.
He also had a fondness for Philistine women, and fell in love
with Delilah when she lived in the valley of Sorek. Delilah means
delicate and dainty one. She was the third Philistine woman with
whom Samson became involved. When his first wife failed to
give the Philistines information that they wanted to render him
powerless, the Philistine lords refused to give up. They also were
aware of Samson's fondness for the Philistine women.

When the lords of the Philistines learned about Delilah, they
went to her with a proposition. "Find out everything you can about

his strength and how we can control him, and we will each give you 1100 pieces of silver." In today's economy, this would add up to $704.00 from each of the five lords, making a total of $3520.00. In that day, with that much silver, she would be considered a very rich woman indeed. This was just too good to pass up, so she accepted the proposition. She was motivated by greed.

Delilah began to pester Samson about his strength. After all, she was now his wife and had a right to know everything about him. She used her feminine wiles on him because she was determined to get the money that they promised her. Samson thought he was smart. After all, he had been through this before with his first wife. He knew what she was trying to do, so he told Delilah his first lie regarding his strength. She followed his instructions and bound him with the seven green bowstrings from animal guts that the lords had given her. Then she said, "The Philistines be upon thee, Samson." He then broke the bowstrings with his strength. Delilah was upset because she felt that he was making fun of her. She did not like this at all, and decided to try a new tactic.

Again Samson told her another lie. This time he told her that if he was bound with new ropes that had never been used, he would be as weak as any other man. She did what he told her to do and again said, "The Philistines be upon thee, Samson." Samson got up again and broke the ropes as if they were pieces of thread. Delilah was really upset now. She thought that she could get any man to do anything she wanted, using her craftiness. After all, she had her beauty to use as her weapon. Samson was really enjoying himself. Delilah kept pestering him until he told her another lie. This time he told her to weave his hair with the web of the loom. This was a more difficult test of strength. She followed his instructions and again said, "The Philistines be upon thee, Samson." He woke from his sleep and broke the loom.

Delilah pestered and pestered him. She was a deceitful and heartless woman with honey on her lips. Four times now Delilah had called in the Philistines to take him. She continued to cry and nag Samson until he tired of listening to her. He finally told her that his hair had never been cut because of his religious belief. If his hair was shaved off, then he would lose his strength. Delilah looked into his eyes and she knew that this time he was telling her the truth. She sent for the lords and told them to come and to bring her money with them, because this time it would happen. Samson would be as weak as any other man.

She was very sweet to him now. She made him relax, telling him all of the things that she knew he wanted to hear. With these enticing words, she placed his head on her lap and soothed him until he went to sleep. When she was sure that he was in a deep sleep, she called for a man to come in and cut off his hair. For the last time she said, "The Philistines be upon thee, Samson." Samson tried to use his strength, but he was as weak as any other man. The Philistines took him and Delilah took her silver. She had finally won.

What questions would you like to ask her?

QUESTIONS:

John: Being the type of person that you are, what would you consider as one of your own strengths?

Delilah: My main strength is that I am persistent. When I see something that I want, I go after it until I get it. It does not matter what I have to do to get it, or whom I hurt in the process. I want it, so it's mine. I know how to use my feminine wiles on any man. I can be sincere one minute and scornful the next. I am a deceitful person and I know it, but I just can't seem to help myself. I must have what I want. The harder I must strive to get it, the more I want it and the more persistent I become. This is just the real me.

Maria: Why do you think Samson let you use him like you did? Do you feel that he knew what you were trying to do to him?

Delilah: Yes, I feel that he knew all the time. He is just like any other man. I don't believe he felt that I was using him. He really thought that he could outsmart me. He took it as a game. That is why he lied to me four times. He figured that I would stop trying, but he had met his match. All I could think about was the money.

Kent: The Bible mentions that you committed seven sins. What were they?

Delilah: I entered into an agreement with the lords of the Philistines to commit sin. I committed adultery. I performed evil for money. I used deception while plotting the death of a man who professed to love me. I took advantage of Samson's love to betray him to his enemies. I also took advantage of him at his weakest moment, while he was asleep, to destroy him. And, finally, I was warring against God and seeking to overthrow the anointed one (Samson) whom He had raised up to deliver Israel.

Alice: Was there anything about Samson that you liked?

Delilah: I like men to be strong in a manly way. Samson was physically strong and was able to do many wonderful feats, but that was all. He was a challenge but, once I got to know him, he was just putty in my hands. It makes me feel good when I bring so-called big strong men to their knees. He tried to be more than he really was. I don't like any man to feel that he is so much smarter than I am. They have to learn that when they tangle with me, they have met their match. Samson was just too full of himself, and I had to bring him down.

Kent: How did you know when Samson was telling you the truth?

Delilah: I studied men. I have been with so many men that I can usually tell when they are lying to me. I let them say what they want to say, and then I pester them until they begin to see things my way. It also shows in their eyes. When they think they are putting one over on you, their eyes sort of light up and they look away. But when they tell you the truth, they look right into your eyes because they have nothing to hide. I had pleaded, begged, nagged, and cried so much, and I knew that sooner or later, Samson would tire of me. Most men can only take so much from a woman, especially one that he thinks he loves.

Irene: Why was money so important to you? In your day, women did not have much authority over their lives, so there was really not much that you could do with it.

Delilah: I know that I was limited in my activities as a woman. Women in my day were only for decoration, and used to do the bidding of men. I didn't mind this, because I was getting good pay. I might not be able to do anything big with the money, but just the knowledge that I had it was enough. Think of the prestige that I had. All that money, no bills, everything that I need is taken care of by someone else. What more could a girl want or need?

Kellie: You have been called many things, temptress, seductress, deceitful, harlot, evil, etc. Some Bibles have made a reference in Proverbs 5:3-4 ("For the lips of a strange woman drop as a honeycomb, and her mouth is smoother than oil: But her end is bitter as wormwood, sharp as a two edged sword") KJV. How does this make you feel?

Delilah: My goal in life was to get as much wealth as I could. What other people called me did not bother me. What other people thought of me did not bother me. I know who I am and what I stand for. Yes, I was a temptress; I used my feminine wiles when I needed to. I also used sex when necessary. As long as I was getting what I wanted, it did not matter. You see, I knew what I wanted in life. I had only one goal in mind, and I was determined and persistent in obtaining that goal. I did very well too if I may say so myself.

The life that I lived was not a good life. At the time though, I thought that I had it made. What I wanted, I got. There were many things that I did not need, but I was greedy. At the time, I enjoyed everything that I was involved in, especially when I was making money. But as I look back over my life, I realize that I was not really happy. I was trying to compensate for my unhappy existence by taking it out on others, especially the men. Whatever I could do to get the best of men, I did, and I felt like I was really something. But, ultimately, I died when Samson destroyed the temple. I was still young and beautiful. I did not even get a chance to enjoy the money that I had earned.

Alice: What advice would you give us today?

Delilah: I would suggest the following:

- Be true to yourself. My problem was that I was not true to myself. I wanted to be rich and admired. I knew I was beautiful and I flaunted it. Men knew I was beautiful and lusted after me. I knew they wanted me. I would parade in front of them, drawing attention to myself, so that they would desire me. Samson was no different. I had heard about the things he had done with his great strength. I also knew of his preferences for foreign women. Then there was the money. I had beauty, but I was not satisfied. I had to be rich. When the lords offered me that money, I grabbed it. I destroyed a good man because of my vanity and my greed. I was not being true to myself. What I really wanted was someone to love me for whom I was, someone who admired me because of my vanity, but strong enough to deal with my idiosyncrasies. I never let a man get close enough to me to know who I really was. (For everyone who

Quinn Morris, Psy.D.

exalts himself will be humbled [ranked below others who are honored or rewarded] and he who humbles himself [keeps modest opinion of himself and behave accordingly] will be exalted [elevated in rank]. Luke 14:11 Amplified)

- Women, use your cunning wisely. You are very capable of making or breaking a man. If you find a man who really loves you, don't take advantage of him. Treat him with respect, and demand that he in turn show you respect. Accept his love and love him in return. Work with him to make and keep your relationship positive. You can take a man down or you can build him up. Do the latter. (The wise woman builds her house, but with her own hands the foolish one tears her's down. Stay away from a foolish man, for you will not find knowledge on his lips. The wisdom of the prudent is to give thought to their ways, but the folly of foolish is deceptive. Proverbs 14:1, 7-8 NIV)

- Men, use your skills wisely. Treat your woman as you would want to be treated. Treat them as equals and have that same expectation from them. Don't take advantage of them and don't let them take advantage of you. Men, you also can take a woman down or build her up. Do the latter. (A simple man believes anything, but a prudent man gives thought to his steps. A wise man fears the Lord and shuns evil, but a fool is hotheaded and reckless. A quick-tempered man does foolish things, and a crafty man is hated. Proverbs 14:15-17 NIV)

- Learn all you can about yourself. If you are not sure who you are, take some time and get to know who you are. Write down your likes, dislikes, beliefs, goals, etc., everything you can about yourself. Ask your family members and friends what they think of you. Get as much information about yourself as possible. It can be very informative, as well as an excellent way to get to know what others who are close to you think about you. A comparison of everyone's list helps you learn a lot about who you really are. (Whoever loves discipline loves knowledge, but he who hates correction is stupid. The plans of the righteous are just, but the advice of the wicked is deceitful. Proverbs 12:1, 5 NIV)

• Respect others for their beliefs. You do not have to agree with what they believe, how they worship, or who they worship, just respect them and their beliefs. (Therefore, if [my eating a] food is a cause of my brother's falling or of hindering [his spiritual advancement] I will not eat [such] flesh forever, lest I cause my brother to be tripped up and fall and to be offended. I Corinthians 8:13 Amplified)

BIBLIOGRAPHY

Lockyer, Herbert: All the Women of the Bible, Zondervan Publishing House, Grand Rapids, Michigan, 1967. (If needed)